NORSE PAGANISM FOR BEGINNERS

THE COMPLETE BEGINNER'S GUIDE TO LEARN
ABOUT NORSE MYTHOLOGY, MAGIC, RUNES,
AND THE WORLD OF NORSE RELIGION

ODIN KELTOI

PUBLISHING FORTE

INTRODUCTION

The world we live in comprises many different types of religions from all over the globe. According to a rough estimate by the experts, there are about 4000 religions globally. Each religion is different from the other in one way or another. People learn about specific religions from their forefathers, parents, and other people. They usually follow it for the whole of their lives. However, sometimes they start thinking rationally and switching to another religion. Anyhow, it is the freedom of the people worldwide that they can choose the religion that answers their queries in the best possible manner.

If we talk about some of the most popular religions from ancient history, the name Norse Paganism will always be given a special place on the list. Defining it in simple terms is a religious movement related to pre-Scandinavian traditions and beliefs. The Norse Religion may be traced back to the Iron Age Germanic peoples, and its development continued till the Reformation of Scandinavia.

The people of today have a lot of confusion in their minds as far as the Norse religion is concerned. They want to know about the roots of the religion to comprehend its teachings in a better manner. Similarly, they also want to know about the total number of gods present in the Norse Pagan religion of the past. In the same way, they want to understand whether religion is still in practice anywhere in the world or not. Many people believe that with the arrival of Christianity, the old Norse religion – the belief in Norse gods – died out. However, it did not and was instead practiced in secret or under a Christian shroud.

The book Norse Paganism for Beginners is a comprehensive package for all the interested learners as it is understandable by the name. Speak about any concept of complexity related to this specific religion and you will see it explained properly in different chapters of the book. The main aim is to let people from the modern-age know about all the core concepts of the religion to draw precise comparisons with other religions.

First, you will come across the history and origin of the Norse religion as it is the most important part of the study if you want to completely understand all the things. The books from the past suggest that religion is as old as the 9th century and it finds its origin in the Scandinavian countries of the world. Old Norse Religion, often called Norse Mythology, is by far the most frequent name for a school of Germanic religion that arose in the era of the Proto-Norse time frame when the Germanic communities split off into their group.

Once you go through the history and origin part in detail, the next part will be waiting for you with even more interesting concepts and stories from the past. All of the tales described in the book are directly or indirectly related to the religion of the Pagans. In the next part of the book, you will be able to learn about the fundamental concepts of the religion under discussion. It is vital to know about the core ideology of the Pagans if you want to have a clear comprehension of what religion is all about. In the same chapter, you will also encounter the practices observed in the Norse Mythology over an extended period. Getting the information about the total number of Gods of Norse Paganism and precise descriptions will help you clear all the related queries from your mind.

The book also gives a special place to the association of the bible and Paganism to help readers get all the core insights into the mythology.

It is crucial to mention here that Gods and Goddesses hold a special place in the Norse Paganism and the discussion about it would be termed incomplete without mentioning all of them in detail. It is a religion with multiple gods, and each God has its qualities and exclusive traits.

Readers who feel like becoming pagans for their good can adopt the religion by using a few simple steps and making minor changes to their routine lifestyle. Becoming a pagan is answered with the proper explanation that can be of extreme help for beginners. It is important to identify the reasons that compel you to follow Norse Paganism. If you have done enough rational thinking and are willing to give it a go, the book Norse Paganism for Beginners is a must-read for you.

Like multiple Gods and Goddesses, Norse Mythology is also full of magic tales, runic alphabet mechanisms and spell jars. The readers who even have a slight interest in magic and other such things can get a lot of information in the book and proper references from the origin of such a mythology. For example, Seir was a sort of sorcery performed in Norse civilization during the Old Scandinavian Iron Age, according to Old Norse. The practice of seir is thought to be sorcery that has to do with foretelling and to shape the future.

Do you think that the religion we are talking about is still practiced today or not?

Such a question should not be bothering you anymore as enough light is being thrown on this particular topic so that the readers can compare it with the religions of today.

Last but not least, all the discussion and information present in the book is highly authentic and nothing is made-up on our own to have the attention of our readers. Norse Paganism for Beginners is a comprehensive book for people who want to learn everything about the authentic religion. So, without thinking and pondering about your questions related to Paganism anymore, switch to the first chapter and gain all the desired knowledge in a single go.

WHAT IS NORSE PAGANISM?

We live in a world with several religions from all over the world. Most of these religions originated quite a few centuries ago. The same goes true for the Norse Paganism religion. However, it still has several followers all over the globe and there are multiple debates about whether it is present in its original state or not. To know more about Norse Paganism, you can go through the below-stated information.

History of Norse Paganism

Old Norse Religion, often called Norse Paganism, is the most frequent designation for a component of Germanic religion that arose during the Proto-Norse era when North Germanic peoples split off into their groups. During the era of the Christianization of Scandinavia, it was superseded by Christianity and forgotten. Scholars use ancient language, anthropology, toponomy, and artifacts left by North Germanic tribes. It includes runic writings in the Younger Futhark, a characteristically North Germanic variant of the runic alphabet, to recreate parts of North Germanic religion. Norse mythology, a part of North Germanic religion, is documented in several Old Norse literature dating from the 13th century.

Old Norse implied that different gods and goddesses were worshipped. In Norse mythology, these gods were separated into two groups: who were thought to have participated in an ancient conflict until they realized they were both equally powerful. Odin and Thor were two of the most widely worshipped gods. Other fabled races, such as titans, dwarfs, elves, and land-spirits, also lived on this planet. The world tree Yggdrasil was central to Norse cosmology, with different worlds, including Midgard, residing alongside humanity. There are various afterlife realms, each governed by a different deity.

Old Norse religion, which was passed down by oral tradition rather than written scriptures, placed a strong emphasis on ritual practices, with monarchs and leaders playing a key part in public sacrifices. Various cultic places were employed; initially, outdoor spaces like groves and lakes were preferred, but cult homes appear to have been built for ritual activity after the third century CE, though they were never widely used. Practitioners of Seir, a sort of magic that some researchers define as shamanistic, were also found in Norse society. In addition to inhumation and cremation, several types of burials were carried out, usually followed by various grave artifacts.

Throughout its history, neighboring peoples such as the Sami and Finns have experienced varying degrees of trans-cultural diffusion. Old Norse mythology had surrendered to Christianity by the twelfth century, with remnants of it surviving in Scandinavian folklore. During the nineteenth century's romanticist movement, there was a surge of recognition of the Old Norse religion, which inspired various artworks. It drew the attention of politicians and was utilized by a variety of right-wing and nationalistic organizations. The study of Paganism started in the early 19th century, driven by the widespread romanticist feeling of the period.

Origins in the Iron Age

Old Norse religion, according to Andrén, was a "cultural patchwork" that arose from a variety of older Scandinavian religions. While the supposedly solar-oriented religion framework of Stone Age Scandinavia is thought to have faded out at about 500 BCE, a variety of Bronze Age themes as the wheeled cross—reappear in subsequent Iron Age contexts. It is frequently thought to have evolved from older religious belief systems among some Germanic Early Medieval peoples. The Germanic languages are considered to have originated in what is now northern Germany or Denmark during the first millennium BCE and then expanded throughout Europe. Many of the gods in Old Norse mythology have counterparts in other Germanic communities. About 500 to 400 BCE, the Scandinavian Iron Age began.

The importance of archaeological data in comprehending these early periods cannot be overstated. According to researcher Gabriel Turville-Petre, Tacitus wrote accounts from this period, and his insights "assist in understanding" subsequent Old Norse religion. According to Tacitus, the Germanic peoples had priests, open-air holy locations, and a strong emphasis on human sacrifice, ritualists, and fortune-telling. Tacitus mentions the polytheistic nature of the

Germanic peoples, and some of their gods are referred to as Roman equivalents.

The Expansion of the Viking Age

Norse people departed Scandinavia during the Middle Ages and settled in other parts of Northwestern Europe. Some of these territories were sparsely populated, including Britain, Southwestern Wales, Scotland, the Isle of wight, Isle of Man, and Ireland, which were already densely populated.

Norwegian people departed their homeland in the 870s to populate Iceland, carrying their religious beliefs with them. Although there are saga records of devotees of Freyr, along with a "priest of Freyr" in the subsequent Hrafnkels saga, place-name evidence implies that Thor was the most prominent God on the island. There seem to be no place names associated with Odin on the island. Unlike other Nordic civilizations, Iceland was without a monarchy and hence a centralizing authority that could enforce religious devotion; yet, from the time of its initial colonization, there were both pagan and Christian communities.

In the late ninth century, the Old Norse religion was brought to Britain by Scandinavian invaders. For example, British place names like Roseberry Topping in West Yorkshire were identified as Othensberg in the eleventh century, indicating possible cultic sites. Old Norse connections to mythological entities can also be found in place names. To Christianize this arriving population, the English Church needed to conduct a fresh conversion process.

Christianity's Rise and Fall

The Nordic region first encountered Christianity through colonization in the (previously Christian) British Isles and commercial links with eastern Catholics in Novgorod and Byzantium. Christianity had already been the accepted religion throughout most of Europe by the time it arrived in Scandinavia. Because there are no textual depictions of this conversion process comparable to Bede's depiction of the earlier Anglo-Saxon conversion, it is unclear how Christian organizations converted these Scandinavian settlers. The Scandinavian migrants, on the other hand, appear to have switched to Catholicism within the first few years of their arrival. After Christian missionaries from the British Isles traveled to northern Europe in the eighth century, Charlemagne tried to push for Christianization in Denmark, proselytizing in the kingdom during the ninth century. Harald Klak, the Danish monarch, converted to Christianity in 826, most likely to strengthen his political relationship with Henry the Pious over his competitors for the throne. Under Horik II, the Danish royalty returned to the Old Norse religion.

In England, the Norwegian monarch Hákon turned to Christianity. When he returned to Norway, he kept his beliefs mainly private but urged Christian clergymen to preach among the people; this enraged some pagans, and three cathedrals built on the site of Trondheim were burned down, according to Heimskringla. Harald Greycloak, his successor, was also a Christian, but he had limited success in persuading the Norwegian people to accept his faith. While he consented to be baptized under the duress of the Danish king and permitted Christians to evangelize in the realm, Haakon Sigurdsson actively supported pagan sacrificial traditions, asserting the supremacy of old deities and encouraging Christians to return to their adoration. During his reign (975–995), a "state paganism" emerged as an official ideology that fused

Norwegian and pagan identities and united sympathy behind Haakon's leadership.

After Haakon died in 995, the next king, Olaf Tryggvason, assumed control and actively promoted Christianity, forcing elevated Norwegians to convert, destroying temples, and murdering those he labeled "sorcerers." However, little is documented about the progress of Christianization in Sweden; it is believed that the Swedish monarchs had switched by the eleventh century and that the nation was Christian by the 12th century.

Olaf Tryggvason dispatched a brand, a Saxon missionary, to Iceland. Angbrandr's proselytizing enraged many Icelanders, and he was banished after slaying numerous poets who ridiculed him. On the island, hostility among Christians and pagans intensified, and both parties rebuked each other's gods at the Althing in 998. To keep the country united, the Althing in 999 agreed that Icelandic legislation would be established on Christian ideas, with some allowances for the pagan population. Pagan offerings and rituals were permissible in private, albeit not in public.

Conversion to Christianity was tightly linked to social ties across Germanic Europe; mass conversion, rather than individual conversion, was the norm. The desire for help from Christian monarchs, whether in money, imperial sanction, or military support, was a significant motivator for kings to convert. The polytheistic nature of Old Norse religion permitted its practitioners to accept Jesus Christ as one deity among many, making it difficult for Christian missionaries to persuade Norse people that the two belief systems were mutually exclusive. The interaction with Christianity may also inspire new and innovative forms of pagan culture, such as by influencing numerous ancient mythologies. Pre-Christian beliefs are more likely to have survived in remote locations, while others have remained in folklore.

The Age of Transformation Has Arrived

In Scandinavia, the Vikings Age was a time of significant religious transformation. The prominent perception of the Vikings is that they would be all pagans who despised the Christian Church, yet this perception is incorrect. The whole populace of Scandinavian was pagan at the start of the Middle Ages. Still, the Vikings had numerous gods, and accepting the Christian deity alongside their own was not a difficulty for them. Most historians now assume that Viking raids on Christian churches were inspired by the fact that monks were often wealthy and poorly protected, making them an attractive target for loot.

Through their raids, the Vikings came in contact with Christianity, and when they remained in countries with a Christian populace, they rapidly converted. It was applicable in Brittany, Ireland, and the British Isles. We can see from the archaeological sites that even though contemporary narratives speak little about it. Pagans buried their deceased with grave goods, whereas Christians did not, making the shift in religion easy to detect.

As White European and German preachers came to Scandinavia to convert the pagans, the Viking Age saw a slow conversion in Scandinavia itself. By the mid-eleventh century, Christianity had taken root throughout Denmark and the majority of Norway. Although there was a transient conversion in Stockholm in the 11th century, Christianity was not established until the mid-12th century. Christians took seized traditional pagan sites as part of the conversion process.

Gamle Uppsala is a notable example of this, with the ruins of a history of the church standing amid a series of massive pagan burial mounds.

The Basics of Norse Paganism

Heathenry is a contemporary neo-pagan religion influenced by pre-Christian Northern European cultures' folkloric rituals, customs, beliefs, and worldviews. Heathens are people who follow the Heathen religion. Norse Heathenry is also known as Norse Mythology, Astro, or Forn Sir/Forn Sed, a subset of Heathenry.

As the name implies, Norse Polytheism is a modified form of old spiritual beliefs and practices held by the antiquity Norse people. When we speak of the Norse, we usually think of "Vikings," although it was a specialized occupation, and not all Germanic individuals were Vikings. The Norse were ordinary people with different occupations, lifestyle choices, and values. They had in common culture, which was where their spiritual practices came from.

Norse Heathenry is a decentralized religion, which means that there is no "central" authority or basic dogma. This is due to the lack of religious texts, scriptures, or major religious personalities to guide practices and beliefs and doctrines, creeds, and dogmas in Heathenry.

For something called "religion," this may appear strange. When most of us speak of "religion," we usually think of popular religions.

There are not many high-demand observances in

Heathenry. Old Norse religions emerged naturally from their cultures through family/group/regional traditions, oral history, superstitions, and folklore. These were all unique in terms of location and time. Modern Heathenry differs from one person to the next, from one group to the next, and from one place to another.

Old books containing Norse mythology are not holy scripture, notwithstanding their historical and mythological value. Scripture is a type of text intended to develop religious practice, belief, and community, and it is frequently regarded as divinely inspired. The Eddas were composed by Christian long after Scandinavia had turned to Christianity. In addition, the Eddas only represent a localized interpretation of Myth and folklore, rather than what the entirety of Scandinavia thought at the time. Some Norse Heathens, particularly the Hávamál, gain psychic relationships from these Eddas and their sections, but this is essentially a matter of personal taste.

Animistic

Animism is the belief that all objects in existence have activity because no one item is more important than the others. When you look at things through an animistic lens, you realize that everything has a role within the interrelated system it lives in—not because of any moral objective or purpose, but because it exists. Things ought to be respected for what they are, and by doing so, we can cultivate a spiritual approach to the world.

Because of the nature of animism, there is no obvious distinction between sacred and profane in the Norse Pagan worldview. The divine is a part of our world as colors, sounds, and physical substance; it is a quality of existence, not a condition to attain or a presence to earn. As a result, in Norse Paganism, there is no such thing as "sin," because deeds do not bring you nearer or even further away from God.

Some define animism as the notion that everything has a "soul" or "spiritual essence," however, this depends greatly on how these terms are defined subjectively. Nevertheless, many Norse Heathens feel that we may sense the metaphysical aspects of our environment, resulting in the following common lore in Norse Paganism Heathenry: We can build bonds with our deceased forefathers and mothers. Land-vaetter ("land-spirits") inhabiting the land, trolls inhabiting large rocks and pebbles, Nisse and husvaetter ("house-spirits") inhabiting living areas, Jötunn as manifestations of the wild-ness, and the Aesir—our divinities expressions of the phys-ical world and people. Plus, we have complete control over how we engage with these objects.

Heathens like participating in these things in the same manner that we enjoy engaging with one another; these interactions generate a feeling of attachment and lend a ritual component to our engagement in nature. However, how this is accomplished differs from person to person.

Pluralistic

Religions are founded on a variety of philosophies. The way these things psychologically relate to each other is one idea that religions attempt to address.

HEATHENRY IS A PLURALISTIC RELIGION. It thinks that objects are made up of many parts, are based on many principles, and include various, multiple, or even moving truths. This contrasts with dualistic (two principles) and monotheism (one principle).

Dualist religions include Christianity and Wicca. Things are classified as "good" or "evil" in Christianity, and this distinction is the topic of constant strife in the world. For example, the "divine male" and "divine feminine" are seen as having opposites in Wicca, and this dualism should be respected.

One illustration of a monotheistic belief is pantheism. Everything, it argues, is a manifestation of one thing: The Universe. "The core of all things originates from one vitality or spiritual origin, according to the New Age notion of "Source."

HEATHENRY IS PLURALISTIC, so it doesn't see persons, things, or forces as "good" or "bad," It doesn't believe in a single guiding factor. Dualist and monist notions may occasionally appear in Heathenry, but they present problems when applied to beliefs or attitudes that are not supported by pluralism.

Polytheistic
The belief in numerous gods is known as polytheism. Heathenry, notably Norse Heathenry, is polytheistic. The Norse Gods and Goddesses are numerous. Some are well-known characters, such as Odin, Loki, Freyja and Thor, while some are relatively unknown. The Norse pantheon, like the remainder of Heathenry, was never centralized, Therefore, different gods have varying levels of support in different eras and places. A seaside town in Scandinavia would worship Njord or gir, while a mountainous settlement might worship Skadi and Ullr.

Immanent

Religion or spirituality might fall into two categories: intrinsic faith of transcendent faith. It may be a combination of the two.

IMMANENT FAITHS ARE CONCERNED about the quality, self-actualization, and fulfillment of our contemporary lives and our interaction with the environment around us. Our present reality, wellness, and life experiences are at the centre of our practices and observances.

Norse Heathenry exemplifies immanent faith. Our main focus is on the animism experience and the connections we form about ourselves and others. To have a nice afterlife, practitioners are not obligated to lead their lives in a certain way. Many of us believe that we will immediately rejoin our relatives unless we want to pursue something different, such as an eternity in Valhalla, wherein there are rules about how we live and die. However, it is something we choose to do rather than what we are obligated to do as Heathens.

Transcendent faiths emphasize transcending current reality. Each faith has its way of doing this and why it is done is quite obvious. Concepts like illumination and soul ascent are central to transcendent philosophy. Sublime faiths may also place a strong emphasis on the future and how to achieve a good one.

Christianity is an illustration of a faith that is transcendent. In Christianity, all personal decisions and acts either move somebody closer to Heaven or further away from God, determining whether they go to Heaven after death.

Doctrines and dogmas decide what activities are used to accomplish this.

Norse Heathenry is mostly an intrinsic religion, but it does contain some transcendent components. The notion that all those who perish in combat travel to Odin's hall, Valhalla, is the most apparent example. The völva's labor and the berserker's frenzy are two more possible instances. On the other hand, these transcending aspects are elective rather than mandatory. We have the option of incorporating transcendent philosophies into our practices.

The Bible and Norse Paganism

Asatru is a present-day neo-pagan restoration of Old Norse, which was before in line with its religious framework that has risen in popularity in many nations over the last fifty years, particularly in Europe and North America.

ASATRU IS the name given to the modern restoration of Scandinavian religious traditions before the arrival of Christianity by adherents of the Scandinavian neo-pagan faith in the 19th century.

The name translates roughly to "to be true to the sir," one of the Norse god clans represented in Norse mythology.

Asatru intended to be true to the Norse gods overall during the 19th century, to be truthful and worship the Greek gods and their symbols. Still, as knowledge of pre-Christian Scandinavian pagan religions grew, as did the formation of another branch of this pagan faith, Asatru also came to pertain to a religious practice much more focused on the sir tribe of gods.

When did Asatru begin to exist?

Archaeology began to pique the interest of the European nobility in the nineteenth century. Because having such renowned employment as a hobby was exceedingly prestigious, this became an extracurricular activity for the richer segments of society.

AS A RESULT, interest in archaeology flourished. In the 19th-century, countries seeking answers to questions about patriotism and the need to identify a shared history to unify the people and new nations under development looked to archaeology.

People became more conscious of their past because the nineteenth century was a period of great change. With the rising industrialization process and the abdication of cultures and the relatives in balance in favor of continuing to work in highly industrialized manufactures, most people wanted to go back to their roots. They struggled to accept the changes in society brought about by industrialization.

PEOPLE DIDN'T WANT to return to a religious heathen past; instead, they wanted to return to the world, tradition, and domestic and farming occupations that were less stressful and depressing than the new industrial reality. Archaeological and the social desire for tradition and traditional rituals were ultimately brought together.

The historical and archaeological interpretation of

ancient European civilizations was that modern Europeans' ancestors idolized nature. The train of reasoning perfectly fit both the affiliations devoted to awareness of the late nineteenth century and the political ideologies of nationalism – to come back to the land, to be self-sufficient, conservative values and traditions.

Many pre-Christian European societies were viewed as nature worshippers in this way. To some extent, this was true because archaeological interpretations were centered on European cultures from the Neolithic onwards, civilizations whose lifestyles revolved around different seasons – sowing the soils, harvesting the crops, storing food for the winter, and so on.

As a result, it was assumed that pagan European tribes worshiped nature and that most of their divinities were fertility deities. However, during the twentieth century, specifically the early 1970s, individuals and groups from Iceland, the United States, and the British Isles formed a new religious affiliation devoted to the Revival of pre-Christian Northern European religious beliefs and practices, especially those of pre-Christian Iceland and Scandinavian nations, but also the related customs of the Northern people of mainland Europe and the Anglo-Saxons, Satr took on a new significance as it evolved into faith with solid roots and a more defined theological organization.

Asatru is not a very old religion, and it is not even older than Christianity. Asatru is a current neo-pagan religious restoration centered on a collection of faiths and spiritualties derived from pre-Christian Northern European spiritual beliefs.

The Norse forefathers did not call their religion Asatru. Before, Scandinavians did not follow a single religion but a variety of cults that had connections with numerous pre-Christian tribal tribes distributed over Northern Europe.

HEATHENS (an ancient Germanic name for non-Christians) and Heathenry are other terms they use to describe themselves and their religion. Those who are unfamiliar with the term "satr" typically refer to it as "Viking Religion," and it is commonly referred to as "Nature Worship" throughout the faith.

Nationalist minds dominated archaeology in the nineteenth and early twentieth centuries. They were looking for a shared history in each other's countries to serve as a reference point and a component demonstrating that a similar culture previously connected such nations.

The Viking Age was essentially what cemented Scandinavians' place in history. Before the Viking Period, when Scandinavians first exposed themselves to the rest of Europe, nothing was known about the centre.

Archaeology of the Viking Age is a means of discovering a shared culture that once united the Swedes. This actual history was a focal point of political culture in Scandinavia, particularly Norwegian, during the nineteenth century and the early twentieth century. With J.R.R. Tolkien's writings centered on Old Norse and Old English writings, and later with Thor Studies bringing up the Norse tales in the exploits of Thor, the God of thunder, Viking culture became prevalent and very much a trend.

As a result, a religion like Asatru was easily referred to as "The Religion of the Vikings," not only because of its obvious connection to Norse myths and folklore but because of the formation of satr and its basic religious beliefs are mostly focused on Old Norse literary works. Both Sagas and Poems from the Viking Period, or late medieval and early contemporary Scandinavia, portray much of them before Norwegian religious beliefs and practices.

If individuals wish to learn more about Asatru, one of the most common questions they have is whether satr is only for persons of Scandinavian heritage. True, Satr has been dubbed "The Viking Religion," which has led to the assumption that only persons with significant Scandinavian roots are permitted to venerate the Norse gods.

There's also the association with satr of Modernity and far-right political parties. Numerous studies have been done because of the inclination to associate Norse Paganism with racist and Neo-Nazi groups within Nordic Pagan societies.

DESPITE POPULAR BELIEF that Neo-Nazis populate satr, the vast majority of current Nordic Pagans dedicated to Northern European culture and heritage are opposed to fascism and racism. Most modern Nordic Pagans condemn the minority of Nordic Pagan religions with Neo-Nazi and far-right politics as members of groups that most Heathens do not want to associate with. There is an ongoing battle against bigotry and Neo-Nazism within Heathenry.

In truth, since the early 2000s, the number of people who practice Northern European pagan rituals has increased. People are honoring the Norse gods and performing

Northern European pagan customs from all over the world, along with many nations with no cultural similarities to Northern Europe.

In America, Asatru started to promote people to search out their cultural past, but let's avoid any misinterpretation. This is not to say that Nordic Pagans' pride in their ethnic background is tied to bigotry, nor should dedication to Nordic heritage be mistakenly equated with Nazism.

It all started with a simple search for and acceptance of cultural heritage. Today, at least in the UK, satr and other types of Heathenries are more about seeking a religion that conforms to our cultural conceptions than about seeking cultural history. Other people were free to accept the Old Nordic customs due to the growing trend away from organized religion and toward spirituality. Many people from different backgrounds, including organizations, have embraced this faith.

They are primarily guiding routes in how we should live our lifestyles to accomplish greatness and appreciate this world to the fullest, benefiting all that surrounds us. As a result, the gods are frequently seen as a natural part of life and manifest themselves through essence, and we humans have a close relationship with them.

Although it is important to emphasize that we are on our own and only seek help from the gods when all sentient efforts and resources have been exhausted since there is no other alternative, it is because when people worship the Norse gods, it necessitates a gift. So, compromises must be made, mostly in celebrations where the community shares personal objects, food, and drink with the gods, to keep the friendships between the gods and us strong.

What Sets Asatru Apart from Other Faiths?

So, Satr is a neo-pagan different religious reconstruction based on pre-Christian Scandinavian religious and historical characteristics.

HOWEVER, it is crucial to note that followers of this faith strive to communicate with Norse gods while acknowledging that other countries get their gods. Therefore, they do not think their deities are the only legitimate gods.

IT IS THEOLOGY, or rebuilding of religious culture, without the need for a hierarchical system, dogmas, or precious books at its core. As a result, religious activities may undergo significant alterations and interpretations depending on the individual.

2

NORSE PAGANISM FOR BEGINNERS

Norse Paganism is an ancient religion that finds its roots in the old times. Some historians believe it is related to Christianity in one way or another, while the others have a contrasting view. Generally speaking, Norse Paganism is recognized as a religion that has multiple Gods for the worshippers. The chapter will tell you more details about religion.

Fundamental Norse Pagan Beliefs

We know nothing about Viking Age pagan religious practices essentially. While there are rare connections to Paganism in the Viking sagas, largely recorded in Iceland in the 1300s, we must realize that these were recorded down two hundred years just after conversion to Christianity. We know that chiefs served as priests and pagan rituals included horse sacrifices, but we don't know much.

Apart from a few mentions in early poetry, these stories

survived conversion because they could be dismissed as mere myths rather than expressions of religious ideas. The Eddas, beautiful literary masterpieces that depict old pagan traditions as folk stories are the principal sources of proof. There is significant Christian influence here as well. The principal God Odin, for example, was committed to himself after being hung from a tree and wounded in the side with a sword, followed by a type of resuscitation a few days ago - an obvious analogy to Christ's crucifixion.

Despite this, the Eddas contain much information about the gods and their interactions with giants, men, and dwarfs. The one-eyed Odin, the Ancestral spirits, God of war, justice, death, wisdom, and poetry, was the most powerful God. Thor, who was foolish yet very powerful, was arguably the most common God. He was the gods' chief defender against the giants, using his hammer Miollnir, made by dwarfs. He was also thunder's deity, and seamen worshiped him in particular. Thor's hammer amulets were very popular among the Vikings. Frey and Freyja, the deity and goddess of fertility, have also been significant, as were several other lesser gods and goddesses.

Giants were the gods' main adversaries, frequent clashes between both races. Only Thor, among the gods, could equal the giants' power, so the gods had to rely on ingenuity to defeat them. Odin was a master of deception, but the gods turned to Loki, the fire god, whenever needed a truly ingenious strategy. Loki performed many acts that benefitted God, but he also did many things that caused them tremendous harm, and his folly created many of the issues he corrected in the first instance.

Despite the tensions among deities and giants, there had

been a good deal of personal contact, and several gods had romances with giantesses. Loki, who already had three monster kids with his giant wife, was one of them. Hel, his daughter, ascended to the throne of the underworld. Jormunagund, one of the sons, grew to be such a big serpent that he extended all the way all around the planet. Fenris, the other son, was a fierce wolf that feared the gods until he was deceived into letting himself be chained by a magical chain until the end of eternity.

The ultimate conflict of Ragnarok, between both the gods and the giants, was thought to be the end of the world. The giants would have Loki and his offspring on their side. Thor and Jormunagund, who had been feuding for a long time, would murder one another, and Odin would have been murdered either by Fenris wolf, who would then be killed. A fire would engulf the entire globe, killing both the deities and humanity. Nevertheless, only a small number of people from both species would survive to create a new world.

Raids against the Frankish realms and the British Isles resulted in more Christian contact. Although Vikings appear to have kept their beliefs throughout their raiding eras, they were pressured to adhere to Christianity if they wanted to have more amicable relations with Christians. This might occur on a government level, as it did in the 878 Treaty of Wedmore. Guthrum, the Viking leader, was obligated by the pact to join Catholicism.

Because Christians were never allowed to trade with pagans, more or less formalized convention applied to trading. Although not all Scandinavian traders appear to have been required to convert completely, the practice of 'prim-signing' (first-signing) was instituted. This was a midway step, short of baptism but signaling a willingness to adopt Christianity, and it was frequently thought sufficient to permit trading.

The arrival of Viking raiders with Christian neighbors added to the burden. Although researchers dispute the extent of Scandinavian settlement in various sections of the British Isles, many individuals now believe that the Vikings supplanted the original population in any given area. Although some settlers carried their family over from Scandinavia, they frequently took native spouses (or partners). As a result, the offspring of these relationships would grow up in largely Christian homes and may even be raised as Christians. Further intermarriage, combined with the Church's influence, resulted in a total conversion.

Some of Viking York's currency suggests that pagans and Christians may coexist. Rather than the ruler's name, one coin variety forms part of St Peter. This appears to be Christian; however, the last 'I' of 'PETRI' on several of the coins is in the shape of Thor's hammer, and many of these coins also feature a hammer on the back. The message on these coins appears to be that neither Paganism nor Christ was accepted.

Practices in Norse Paganism

In Scandinavia, the Middle Ages used the last battle of Paganism, when plundering and trading pushed followers of a polytheistic religion into touch – and often confrontation – with Christians and Muslims who worshipped a monotheistic God.

Certain manuscripts, like the 'Poetic Prose' (a nameless

compilation of unknown Old Norse poetry) and 'Heim-skringla' by Christian Snorri Sturluson, have carried down what we know about the deities and creation stories of the Vikings.

THE UNIVERSE BEGAN for the Vikings and their predecessors with the two components of temperature changes, with Ginnungagap in the middle, and life began in which the two components met and the Titan Ymir was created.

Buri, the father of Odin, Vili, and Ve, was created when Audhumla the bull suckled the infant Ymir and tasted the ice. These men then murdered Ymir, whose corpse became the globe and his skull became the sky, with one of his brows serving as a barrier between the worlds of giants and men.

Yggdrasill, a massive ash tree with three roots, one in Asgard – the realm of the gods (the Aesir), one in Jotunheim – the realm of the frost giants, another in Niflheim – the world of a dead, stood in the center of this universe. Three wells are located near the tree's roots: Hvergelmir, where Nidhogg (the sea monster that gnawed at the tree's roots) lived; Mmis-brunnr, the origin of knowledge (Odin decided to sacrifice a sight for its bodies of water); and Urdarbrunnr, the Destiny Wall, where the 3 Relevant norms irrigate the forest.

The tree connected the eight Norse homeworlds and was home to various animals, along with an eagle in the topmost branches with a falcon perched between its eyes, exchanged insults with Nidhogg.

In different sections of Scandinavia, different gods appear to have ruled. Odin, for example, was revered in Denmark and Sweden; Thor, except in the area surrounding Trond-heim in Norway, was extensively adorned in all three nations; Tyr was popular only in Scandinavia, and Frey in Scandinavia.

The sanctuary in Sweden, just northwest of modern Stockholm, was one of the most prominent areas of Scandinavian Paganism. It is flanked by the burial sites of ancient kings, who were buried with their dogs, horses, servants, and weapons. Every nine years, during the spring equinox, Adam of Bremen reported the largest ceremony, in which nine male animals were sacrificed.

Adam also mentioned three temple images, Thor, Odin, and Frey, who were slaughtered in periods of famine and sickness, war, and weddings, respectively. Thor was a deity of power that held the Mjollnir hammer. As the deity of battle, Odin was the only one who could determine victory or loss. As the deity of fertility, Frey's depiction included an oversized penis. Odin's female slaves, the Valkyrie, led those soldiers killed in combat to Valhalla, where they feasted in Odin's grand hall until Ragnarok.

Each year, three main religious anniversaries were held: one at the start of summer, one in the fall, and one in the middle of winter. The summer dinner was linked with delivering good prosperity and triumph for the upcoming invading season, and sacrifices were performed accordingly.

Slaves were frequently sacrificed to accompany their owners to Valhalla after his death. Ibn Fadlan, an Arab diplomat, narrates the 922 ritual of a Rus funeral on the Volga's banks, which resulted in the murder of a slave girl who willingly joined her late owner on his death march.

From 825 onward, when Louis deployed priests like Anskar to prospering groups like Hedeby, Christians were converting Viking pagans. The conversion process would take a lengthy time, with monarchs like Harald integrating Denmark into the kingdom of Christians over a century after the first converts. The nations to the northwest continued pagans staunchly, but the ancient gods' fate was written on the wall.

Norse religious worship refers to the pre-Christian religious ceremonies performed by Norse pagan religions in Scandinavia. Norse mythology was a folk religion (rather than an organized religion) with the primary goal of societal survival and regeneration. As a result, the faith was decentralized and attached to the community and family, even though evidence of large national religious celebrations exists. The leaders oversaw society's faith; on a community scale, the leadership would be the family head, and on a national level, the leadership was the king. In the contemporary sense, pre-Christian Swedes had no name for religion. The term sidr, which means custom, is the closest match. This resulted that Christianity being thought of as Nr sidr (the new tradition) during the relevant period, whereas Paganism was regarded as forn sidr (the old custom). Religious practice — sacred deeds, rituals, and deity worship — was at the heart of pre-Christian religion.

Norse religion was never a single entity but rather a collection of connected rituals and beliefs. Although the vast geographical distances between Scandinavian countries resulted in a range of cultural distinctions, people knew one another's customs, poetry traditions, and stories. Sacrifice (blót) had an important role in many of the rites that are still known today, and community eating of sacrificed animal meat, and the consumption of wine or mead, played a significant role in the annual feasts. Other foods, such as grain, were more prone to be substituted in ordinary practice. These sacrifices were meant to ensure reproduction and development. There was a clear separation between personal and public faith at the time, and rituals were thus related to either the household and individual or societal structures.

It is unclear how well the tales matched Scandinavian religious beliefs in pre-Christian periods or how people responded to them in daily life. Because the Christians saw the Nordic ideas as sorcery and devil worship, Christian works on the subject were riddled with misunderstandings and unfavorable bias. Some historical evidence has been uncovered, although it is difficult to interpret without the help of written evidence.

Individual methods of Norse Pagan practice differ widely. They also differ between neighborhoods and even regions. Family practices differ from solo practices; solo practices differ from organizational practices, Icelandic practices differ from Norwegian practices, reconstructionist practices differ from revivalist practices, living traditions differ from reconstructionist practices, etc.

This has always been the case due to Heathenry's decentralized structure. It is a matter of personal desire and situation how practices are reinforced and what they are informed by after that.

Reconstructionism and Revivalism are two different types of Reconstructionism.

. . .

RECONSTRUCTIONISM AND REVIVALISM are two prevalent approaches to Heathenry. Given what we know about the past, Reconstructionism attempts to replicate Old Norse religious rituals as accurately as feasible. Revivalism aims to resurrect Old Norse practices in a current context using modern methods.

Both approaches are necessary for modern-day Heathenry's purity and usefulness. The degree to which a Heathen is Reconstructionist or Revivalist is a matter of personal preference. Both strategies have advantages. Reconstructionism often guides us in the right direction, while Revival fills in the gaps. Many people can now participate in Heathen practices, thanks to Revivalism.

Both can hurt one's look, especially when carried to extremes. Heathenry becomes a high-demand religion when unhealthy Reconstructionism treats the past as gospel and uses historic essentialism to gauge "genuine Heathen practice." Unhealthy Revivalism is misleading or appropriative, misrepresenting modern or stolen practices as "old" traditions. They may also completely misrepresent Norse Heathenry. This distributes erroneous information about Heathenry.

Healthy Reconstructionism considers the needs of current people and the ethics of our day, whereas healthy Revivalism is forthright about new material. Neither perspective of Norse Paganism Heathenry is incorrect.

Early Efforts at Reconstruction

Ideological and methodological difficulties plague early reconstruction efforts. Early Reconstructionism was focused on giving white Germans a feeling of storied national heritage rather than truly and faithfully recreating Old Norse rituals due to the origins of modern Norse Heathenry in German Romanticism. Cultural imperialism and antisemitic and anti-Catholic sentiments were invariably present in these early cases.

Early efforts, however, did not result in a true and successful reproduction of old Norse practices. Rather than a theological framework for a revived religious identity, the Old Norse cultures were employed as an aesthetic foundation for a national identity. Many social constructivist branches of Heathenry have this as an implicit (or stated) purpose.

Surviving Techniques

Surviving Heathen practices may fall outside the categories of either Reconstructionism or Revivalism. Old Norse faiths became syncretized to Christian customs rather than fading out completely. These were passed on from one generation to another in the following centuries, typically familial. These lines produced unique observations not seen in normal Revivalist or Reconstructionist techniques. Galdrastafir is a good example of this kind of thing.

Social Changes

Heathens' social interactions with one another can influence how they approach their practices. These rituals might be personal, familial, community, or cultural.

Solo Workouts

Solo practices are exactly what they sound like: a practice that someone creates for himself. This is a common way for someone just beginning their Heathen practice, and the lone practitioner typically tailors their practice to their specific requirements and tastes. Solo practice is commonly referred to as a "hearth cult" in some pagan ways.

Practices in the Family

Family customs have been passed down through the centuries. These are Heathen customs passed down through the generations, and they may have a long history. Other traditions are relatively fresh, producing a new Heathenry lineage to be carried down.

Practices in the Community

Heathens occasionally seek out groups of people to join and celebrate with, whether at local gatherings or larger organizations. These communities, like many other religions, provide spiritual instruction and services.

Cultural Customs

Various countries have different practice styles. What is culturally acceptable among Heathens in one area may not be acceptable in another. For example, some Heathens in the United States would give themselves spiritual names that show their devotion to a deity (e.g., "Odinsdottir"), yet this is considered disrespectful in Danish culture.

Another example: In Norway, Loki is supposed to be the cause of spilopper (both good and bad tricks), whereas, in Denmark, the nisse is believed to be the cause. As seen from Sweden, massive fires are set along the coastlines of Denmark's Midsummer celebrations.

Norse Pagan Gods

The Norse Pantheon contains a large number of gods. Some are well-known, while others are quite unknown. Many legends, tales, sagas, and myths about the gods have been brought down. The Aesir is the name given to them.

MANY GODS WERE HONORED in Norse culture, and most are still worshipped by Asatruar and Pagans today. The gods were a part of daily life for the Norse and Germanic communities, as they were for many other ancient cultures. They were not just something to talk to in times of need. Some of the most well-known divinities of Norse mythology are listed here.

Baldur, the Light God
Baldur is frequently associated with the death and rebirth cycle due to his link with resurrection. Baldur was gorgeous and dazzling, and all the gods adored him.

Freyja, Goddess of Fertility and Abundance
Freyja is a fertility and abundance goddess from Scandinavia. Freyja might be summoned to aid in birth and conception, help with marital issues, or bestow fertility on the shorelines. She was believed to weep gold tears while wearing gorgeous jewelry called Brisingamen, which symbolized the sun's fire. Freyja is a deity of fertility, prosperity, and war and combat in the Norse Eddas. She also has ties to divination and magic.

ASGARD'S PROTECTOR, Heimdall
Heimdall is a deity of light and the custodian of the

Bifrost Gate, which links Asgard and Midgard in Norse mythology. Heimdall is the gods' guardian, and when the world comes to an end at Ragnarok, he will sound a miraculous horn to warn everyone. Heimdall is always on the lookout, and he will be the last one to fall at Valhalla.

Frigga, the Goddess of Prophecy and Marriage

Frigga was Odin's wife and possessed a tremendous prophesy gift. In other legends, she is shown as weaving the fates of mortals and gods, even though she had no authority over their fates. She is attributed with the formation of runes in various Eddas, but she is known as the mother of God in several Norse stories.

Hel, the Underworld Goddess

Hel is the deity of the underworld in Norse mythology. Apart from those killed in combat and went to Valhalla, she was sent by Odin to govern the souls of the dead. It was her responsibility to decide the fate of anyone who crossed her realm.

The Trickster, Loki

Loki has a reputation for being a trickster. In Prose Edda, he is described as just a "contriver of deception." Even though he does not frequently appear in the Eddas, Loki is typically known as a part of Odin's family. Considering his heavenly or demi-god position, there is a slight indication that Loki had his devotees. In other terms, his primary role was to cause havoc for those other deities, men, and the remainder of the earth. Loki was a shapeshifter that could take on the form of any animal or a person of any gender, and he was continually messing in other people's lives, largely for his entertainment.

Njord, the Sea God

Njord was a powerful sea deity wedded to Skadi, the mountain goddess. The Vanir kidnapped him and took him to the Aesir, and he became a holy man of their mysteries.

ODIN, THE GODS' Ruler

Odin was a shifter that went across the world in various disguises. A one-eyed elderly man was one of his favorite manifestations; the one-eyed man frequently occurs in the Norse Eddas as a bearer of wisdom and insight to heroes. He appears in various works, including the Volsung epic and Neil Gaiman's American Divinities. A group of wolves and crows always followed him, and he rode Sleipnir, a magical horse.

Thor, the Thunder God

Thor has been around for quite a long time, with his tremendous lightning bolt. He is still revered by certain Pagans today. He is usually depicted as having red hair and a beard, and wielding Mjolnir, a magic hammer. He was also regarded as important to the agricultural cycle as the guardian of thunder and lightning. If there is a drought, it is not bad to offer Thor a libation, hoping that the rains will come.

Tyr, the God of War

Tyr (also known as Tiw) is the deity of one-on-one battles. He is a deity of heroic triumph and triumph and a warrior. He is shown as possessing only one hand since he is the only one of Aesir bold enough to lay his hand in Fenrir's.

3

HOW TO BECOME A NORSE PAGAN

L ike all the other religions of the world, it is important to learn everything in detail about the ancient and present-day Norse Paganism. If you are interested in becoming a pagan after getting impressed by the concepts and views of the paganism religion, you need to start from the basics. Becoming a pagan is not that difficult after all and it only requires you to start adopting the below-mentioned practices.

Learn About Gods and Goddesses

People in contemporary Pagan religions are frequently drawn to several of the old gods. While this is not a comprehensive list, it is a decent place to start.

THERE ARE many different deities in the world, and which ones you want to revere will frequently be influenced by the pantheon that your spiritual journey follows. Many contemporary Pagans and Wiccans, on the other hand, define themselves as eclectic, meaning they may worship a god from one faith alongside a goddess from another. We may opt to approach a deity for help with a spiritual working or a problem-solving situation in some instances. Regardless, you will have to sit down and sort things all out. How can you determine which gods to invoke if you will not have a clear, recorded tradition? Here are some pointers on how to work with Deity.

The concept of acceptable worship is a topic that comes up frequently when individuals are educated regarding Pagan and Wiccan faith. There is a huge debate regarding the proper sacrifice to give to the divinities of one's religion and how we must respect them when we do so. Let's discuss the idea of Appropriate Worship. Please remember that "proper or acceptable worship" does not imply that someone tells you what is "right or incorrect." It is just the idea that one must take the time to conduct things–including devotion and options- in line with the god or goddess's expectations and requirements.

MAKING some type of sacrifice or offering to the gods is prevalent in several Pagan and Wiccan traditions. It is important to remember that, given the reciprocating aspect of our connection with the supernatural, it is not a case of "I am giving you this item in exchange for you to grant my wish."

Long ago, our forefathers worshipped their gods. Their pleadings and gifts have been recorded in the inscriptions that adorn Egyptian pharaohs' tombs and the sculptures and writings left for us to study by ancient Greek and Roman philosophers and instructors. We receive information regarding man's need to connect with the Divine from India, China, and other parts of the world. Let's take a look at how prayer is used in modern paganism. Prayer is a deeply personal experience. It can be done in a church, a backyard, a forest, or at a dining table, and it can be done out-loud or silently when you need to pray and state what you want. There is a good chance that someone is paying attention.

Are you curious about certain Celtic world's most important deities? Even though the Celts were made up of people from all around the British Isles or Europe, several of their divinities have become part of current Pagan worship.

Ancient Egyptian gods and goddesses were a complex collection of entities and concepts. Many of the gods and their symbolic values changed along with the culture.

MANY OF THE gods adored by the ancient Greeks are being venerated by Hellenic Pagans today. The gods were a part of daily life for the Greeks, as they were for many other ancient cultures. They were not just something to talk to in times of need.

MANY GODS WERE HONORED in Norse culture and are still worshiped by Asatruar and Pagans today. The gods were a part of daily life for the Norse and Germanic communities, as they were for many other ancient cultures. They were not just something to talk to in times of need.

Many Pagan gods are linked to many aspects of human life, including love, death, wedding, fertility, healing, battle, etc. Others are linked to the moon, the Sun, and various periods of the agricultural cycle. Learn more about the various types of Pagan Gods to decide which ones you would want to work with based on your character and magical objectives.

Follow the Pagan Practices

Heathenry in Norse mythology is a dynamic spirituality. It is a mix of old and new constructions, much like civilizations that have endured for a thousand years. Contrary to popular belief, Norse Heathen's practice does not have to "look old" or use "old objects" to be Norse Heathen. All it takes is to have the same components as all kinds of Norse Heathenry worldwide.

Recognizing and Appreciating Your Values and Morals

What are your priorities? What spiritual beliefs do you hold? Considering what you understand or think about the world, what makes perfect sense to you?

UNLIKE OTHER ELEVATED FAITHS, Norse Heathenry does not mandate morals and values; exploring them is the most important component of building a Norse Heathen practice. Culture, rather than divinity, determines what is right and wrong in this spirituality. That is to say; you will decide what you believe, what your ambitions are, or what the standards are for your individual development and evolution.

Naturally, you won't have thorough knowledge about your values in one afternoon, and they won't stay the same over your life. Perhaps the concept of deciding your ideals is unsettling. Before engaging in a Norse Heathen practice, you do not have a clear concept of your values; all you have to do is acknowledge that you are the one who determines them. And, just as you determine your values, everyone else does as well.

What are the Nine Noble Virtues?

You may have come across the Nine Noble Virtues in your research into Norse Heathenry. Unfortunately, fascist, racist, and white nationalist misappropriation of Norse Heathenry have resulted in these and other related codes. Rather than Norse Heathen values, they represent Völkisch conceptions of Germanic values.

Exploring and Debunking Christian Beliefs

This is crucial for any American interested in Norse Heathenry. Except in Scandinavian countries, the United States has a Calvinist culture, so even if you didn't grow up with the faith, some fairly strict Christian beliefs might have ingrained themselves in your mind.

The breakdown of old thinking will occur throughout your Heathen exploration, much like the formation of your ideals. It also won't be a straightforward procedure. Nonetheless, acknowledging the Christian impact in your life rather than attempting to sweep it under the rug can yield better outcomes with Norse Heathenry.

Identifying Your Requirements and Objectives

What are your expectations from Norse Heathenry? Do you have a sense of your position in the universe? Do you have a sense of belonging to your pre-Christian ancestors? Is there a solution for the afterlife? Is there some sort of connection to Norse gods?

Consider why you want to learn more about Norse Heathenry. What brought you to this location? What, if anything, tempts you to remain? Identifying this can assist you in determining your practice's priorities and areas of interest. Is it the gods? Is it the past? Is there something else going on? Your goals and wants, like your beliefs, may change with time, so be open to them when you recognize them.

Become Acquainted with Norse Mythology

Learning about the Norse gods and their stories is one of the greatest ways to start a Norse Pagan practice. The Icelandic Poetic Odin and Prose Edda are the most prominent sources for these stories.

Many individuals in the Northern countries still grow up hearing god stories like they do fairy tales. Even if we do not have exposure to oral history in North America, we can still seek retellings that elicit the same level of interest.

Understanding Norse Heathenry's Evolution

This is a story about two Heathens. The Norse were the ones who came up with the first. It has been passed down through family traditions, cultural conventions, and folklore. In the decade before Nazi Germany, German antisemites developed the second. It survived into the present era by migrating to another nation after the Third Reich ended. The country in question was indeed the United States.

The legacy of Norse Heathenry lasted long since the last Vikings ship sailed, and it still impacts current events. This is specifically right if you are a citizen of the United States.

Using Veneration Techniques

Veneration can come in a variety of forms. Veneration is a

devotional technique commonly utilized to improve one's practice. Heathens do not all conduct the same adoration rituals, nor do they do so in the same way. Here are a few that are frequently encountered in modern practice.

Altars

Many Norse Heathens worldwide construct altars or shrines inside and/or outside their dwellings. Altars are, at their core, dedicated spiritual spaces that you create in your home. These shrines can be altars to Norse gods and spirits or dedicated locations for your practice. Altars are frequently ornamented with images of honored ancestors or deity imagery. Food, drinks, and other presents are left as sacrifices on the altar. Many Norse Pagans begin their physical practice by putting together an altar.

(SOME MEMBERS of the neopagan community distinguish between altars and shrines, with the former serving as a place for magical practice and the latter serving as a "home" for the deity/spirit/ancestor to whom they are dedicated.)

Acts of Devotion

Many Heathens devote activities to deities as a form of worship or establish a feeling of attachment with that Deity. Performing a work linked with a deity, including Frigg or power for Thor, is an example of a holy act. Other times, these activities take the form of creating art for gods, such as paintings, literature, music, and other forms of expression.

IN MODERN PRACTICE, devotional activities are performed from a place of love rather than necessity. These rituals are intended to elicit a sense of engagement between you and your Deity.

While the term "deity" is used, these actions can also be performed on forefathers and other spirits.

Prayer

Pagans may pray to gods for favors, good fortune, or merely converse or voice their grievances. In Norse Paganism, prayer does not have a set format and is not practiced by all Heathens. However, it is a possibility. If a request is answered, it is customary to present a god with an offering.

Choosing Vacations

In Norse Heathenry, holidays are inconsistent. We can't point to any "official" celebrations for this spirituality because they vary so extensively throughout places. Furthermore, many of these holidays were created in Scandinavian topography and latitude; they often change their identity when transferred to North America. In Iceland, where it is dark for half the year, celebrating the Sun's return makes perfect sense, but it makes no sense in Arizona, where the Sun never sets. This has caused some holiday scurrying in the United States.

INTRODUCTION TO DEITY Relations

The terms "spirit work" and "deity work" refer to the process of creating connections with demons and deities. These are commonly (but not solely) used in paganism and polytheism.

At its essence, polytheism believes in numerous gods. From a soft polytheistic perspective (the notion that gods are archetypes) to a hard polytheistic one, polytheism can be approached various ways. Some polytheists work with only one God while admitting the existence of the others, whereas others work with various gods. Some pagan idols are poly-affiliated, which means they work with several gods from various pantheons.

Many polytheists call themselves "pagans," or people who undertake earth-centered rituals. Because spiritual practices may be adapted to your requirements and worldview, they are a good fit.

Relationships between Christian and Pagan Deities

To begin a relationship with a deity or a spirit, you must first understand these interactions. Our view of divinity in the Western world is profoundly Christianized and colonized, and even if they do not grow up practicing the faith, most Westerners have a Christian perception of God. If you are from the West, you may be thinking of a God/Devotee frame-work in a Lord/Servant relationship.

Expectations

The following are some final miscellaneous deity work expectations:

IT TAKES effort to labor for the gods. Studying, learning new tools, gaining new skills, refining your concepts, and experimenting are all part of the process. It should be between yourself and the God you have a relationship with. No one should operate as a committed "interpreter." This can expose you to a lot of possible harm. If you need help with discernment, it is fine to use the help of a third party, but no other entity should be defining your connection with a god or spirits for you.

You have the option of saying "no." You don't have to offer something to a deity/spirit just because they ask for it. The Deity can be made responsible for their deeds, but because they asked doesn't mean you have to do something you do not want to. Gods can say "no." Gods are not like dolls that you can pull out of a system and play with. They are autonomous beings that make their own decisions, so do not expect them to always do what you expect.

Incompatibility does occur. At times, the demeanor, techniques, and antics may not sit well with you. Recognize when it occurs and make necessary modifications. This could entail taking a break, placing some emotional detachment among you two, or even going your separate ways. It may be perfect if this could be done together to ensure a smooth transition.

Synchronicities and Communication Methods

When a god is trying to gain your attention, they usually do so in ways you can understand. They will often show you rather than tell you who they are, and those who are not willing to show you may be impostors. This communication might take place in a variety of ways. Receiving synchronicities, or "coincidences too strange to be coincidences," is part of this puzzle. These could be interpreted as omens or nightmares. We can use astrology and our Clair senses to connect with our gods and get synchronicities.

Omens

An "omen" is a tangible manifestation of a sign, although receiving one is not always a negative omen, as the phrase implies. On the other hand, omens are unsettling or important in some way. The omens of a god will often, but not always, connect with their connotations. Omens can often take on far more mundane forms while still retaining the strange characteristic of synchronicity. They seem to appear at inopportune times.

It takes practice to tell if something is an omen, particularly when you seek them everywhere. Omens are a "gut feeling" type of experience, and not everything unusual you observe is an omen. These three crows are sometimes the Morrigan heralding her arrival, and sometimes there are just three crows. You can ask a deity to send you signals and omens if you are not sure whether they are attempting to call you or not. If you are still unsure, this can assist you in figuring out who that Deity is.

Dreams

Dreams are another way for deities and spirits to identify themselves unless you have aphantasia. It's time to decide not whether a vision is an important part of the entire on its substance and the emotion it gives you, just as it is with omens. This is also a chance for a deity to show themselves in ways that omens alone might not allow. In the same way that you can request a god to give you omens, you may ask a divinity to offer you dreams if you need additional types of proof.

Clairsenses

We have clairsenses that sense the metaphysical world, just as we have senses that observe the material reality around us. In the pagan community, the term "Godphone" is occasionally used. This concept refers to a direct line of communication for both you and a god that is established via the use of clairsenses.

Everyone has clairsenses, which they can improve with effort. We do not always recognize them because we do not know how to employ them deliberately. People usually have one or very few clairsenses greater than the others; these are the ones you should focus on developing. The practice seems to be the only way to find out the exact one and strengthen them.

Clairsensing is one of the most satisfying forms of deity contact, yet it is also difficult to detect. It is easy to mix your clairsenses with your thoughts, signs of mental disorder, intrusive thoughts, and/or excessive negative self-talk when you are first starting. Always check the information you are getting with a reliable divination method.

Three-fold Rule

The Law of Three is a helpful measurement method for distinguishing synchronicities from random events. It is a coincidence to get one sign, information if you get two, and confirmation if you get three. Gods or spirits that desire your attention, in my experience, are very anxious to make them known and will gladly send you several indications. If you are not sure whether you have gotten a sign from such a god, ask for further information.

Bias Against Confirmation

We are just human, after all. When it comes to discernment, one thing to keep in mind is to avoid confirmation bias. Confirmation bias is the propensity to search for, understand, favor, and remember things that confirm or support one's prior personal opinions or values. In other words, rather than resting your beliefs on evidence, it is the act of discovering proof to substantiate your beliefs.

With divinity and spirit work, it is difficult not to have expectations for specific outcomes, but success demands understanding how to analyze metaphysical data as it comes in. The more you struggle to fight biases, the more genuine your spirit encounters will be, which matters. Use many ways of discernment to assist yourself in receiving a clear message.

Preparation for Metaphysics

Magic is an important aspect of spirit and divinity work because it facilitates spirit engagement. When you begin connecting with the afterworld, the otherworld will also want to engage with you. Spirits have a lot of fun toying with folks who are not expecting it. What do you think about those tales about people using Ouija boards to conjure "demons"? It is usually the result of novices making beginner blunders and spirits taking advantage of the situation. Contrary to popular assumption, Ouija boards are no more harmful than any other kind of divination.

Practice and Veneration

Everyday actions of worship are a feature of devotional polytheism. What all of this looks like depends on your route and the practices you choose to implement along the way. People frequently construct a shrine or altar for their gods or goddesses so that they can offer gifts of food, drink, trinkets, and incense as a display of affection and reverence. The practitioner's preferences determine other sorts of interactions. I have a strong connection with Loki via art, but others may connect with their gods via nature, contemplation, trance, music, and other means. There are numerous tips and suggestions available in various pagan communities to assist you in getting started.

Patrons and Mistresses

Some people worship patron/Matron deities. A devotee's Benefactor is the Deity to whom he or she feels the closest connection. This Deity has a unique role in the lives of that devotee, one that extends beyond a traditional devotional bond. No matter what traits a deity has, a devotee will turn to it for protection, direction, and comfort.

If you wonder, "Who is my Patron/Matron?" Remember that Patron/Matron ties are formed rather than assigned. Wicca is a highly gendered duo-theistic religion with no own divine pantheon. Instead, it invites Wiccans to seek out two gods from other pagan gods to symbolize the divine masculinity and femininity, which will serve as the Patron and Matron of that Wiccan. As a result, the phrases can have distinct connotations in Wiccan communities. You are not essential to have both a Patron and a Matron unless you follow a traditional Wiccan practice.

A Period of Dormancy

You may find it tougher to converse with an entity at times as if they have disappeared without a trace. These are known as "fallow" moments in spirit and deity activity, and they are completely normal circumstances. A fallow period does not imply that a deity has abandoned you or that you have abandoned your ability to contact them. It just indicates you are taking a break, similarly to how a farm must pause for a year to allow its soil to replenish its nutrients. The slumber is only temporary, and your abilities will resurface stronger than before.

Oaths and Promises

Making a formal, honor-bound pledge to a deity is known as oathing. This promise can be fulfilled for various reasons, perhaps at the Deity's request, sometimes not. The devotee, the God, and the circumstances within that relationship all have reasons for swearing oaths and vows.

To work with a deity or want them as your Patron, you don't have to take an oath to them. Oaths should not be accepted as a control mechanism or prestige, and they should not be taken if you are uncomfortable with them.

Paths of Norse Paganism

Norse Paganism comes with many different domains, paths and practices, just like all the other religions in the world. If you are looking to become a pagan yourself, one of the most important things is to learn about the paths of Norse Paganism. The following passage will tell you more about different paths in this regard.

Ásatrú

This religious movement began in the nineteenth century and was recognized by Iceland as an official state religion in 1973. The name means "loyal to the Aesir gods," and it refers to the devotion of the Aesir gods (such as Thor as well as Odin), one of the Norse gods' tribes.

Because this is a community-based religion, individuals must act in the community's best interests. This path's organizations are known as "Kindred," their priests & priestesses are known as "Gothar" or "Gythia" (feminine), and their followers are known as "Folk."

Vanatru

The name means "loyal to the Vanir," It first surfaced in the early 1990s as a replacement for satr among individuals drawn to the Vanir gods. The Vanir are indeed the gods & goddesses of fertility, life cycles, and magic; hence witchcraft, folk magic, divination, and nature are central to this path.

IN ADDITION, gods & goddesses are viewed as individuals, with unique rites and ways of communicating with them, as opposed to satr, where all rituals and offerings are the same.

Rökkatru

Abby Hellasdottir invented the phrase "loyal to the Rökkr." In Norse mythology, the Rökkr are the "dark" deities and the Jotun, or giants (for example, Hel, Loki, or Jörmungandr). Death, chaos, and ancient elements like ice and fire are all represented.

DARKNESS OR DISORDER does not equate to evil for the Rökkatru as it does in Catholicism. Instead, they are acknowledged as a necessary part of life's cycles, and they, too, deserve to be worshipped. This is not to say that you cannot worship other deities, but it is necessary to comprehend all aspects of them.

Unlike Satr, this path is tied to Norse Shamanism and focuses on the individual's development and personal relationship to the deities.

CREATION

The Eddic legends attest to Norse Paganism's genesis myth. Ginnungagap, a limitless stretch of barrenness, is the starting point for this myth. Niflheim, a wasteland of cold fog on one half of the void, and Muspelheim, a blazing inferno of flames on the other. They came together to become Ymir, the first giant, and Auumbla, the cosmic cow. Ymir grew to enormous proportions thanks to the cow's milk, and Auumbla ate the saline rim of Ginnungagap for sustenance.

Ymir slipped into a deep slumber at one point. The first male and female jötunn sprang from his armpits, and a six-headed troll erupted from his thighs. These beings swiftly produced their progeny.

Odin and his other brothers killed the gigantic Ymir. Except for Bergelmir & his wife, who escaped by boat, his body poured so much blood that it smothered every jötunn and troll. The universe was subsequently fashioned from Ymir's body by Odin and his brothers; his blood formed the oceans, the land, his skeleton the hills, and his teeth the stones and bounders. Ymir's eyelashes separated Midgard (Earth) and Jötunheim. The brothers crushed Niflheim underneath and divided Muspelheim's fires into several locations, including the sky, which became stars. The heavens, kept above by four dwarves named Norri, Suri, Austri, and Vestri, are made up of Ymir's brains and his skull.

The gods of Aesir convened an aging (council) to define the locations of the planets and the passing of days, months, and years. The heat from the Sun and the rain that fell throughout time gave life to the world's grass, trees, and plants. Animals and spirits of all kinds soon began to populate the world.

Odin and his siblings traveled down the seashore one day when they stumbled across ash and an oak tree. They produced the first man and woman, Ask and Embla, from these. Odin handed them the soul's breath, and the siblings handed them a gift. They were given spirit, thought, and/or will by Hoenir/Vili. Vé/Lour gave them life, emotion, and a vibrant complexion. Ask and Embla moved on to have a large family, giving birth to a large number of people.

THE AFTERLIFE and Death

Dying and the afterlife in Norse mythology are possibly the only well-known aspects of Heathenry and the most misunderstood.

Many people know Odin's hall, Valhalla, where selected warriors who die in combat feast and spar until Ragnarök summons them to fight. Valhalla's depiction in mainstream culture renders it seems like Norse heaven, to the extent where some Heathens consider Valhalla to be the ultimate destination.

IN ACTUALITY, the Norse Pagan concept of death is far more nuanced and varied than the clichés prevalent in the media.

Norse Heathenry is a real religion, or what theologians refer to as an immediate faith. This is a spiritual perspective that stresses the experience of life and well-being over after-life worries. On the other hand, a transcendent faith concentrates on achieving a specific destiny or ascension afterlife.

The Dorms of the Afterworld are a set of corridors that lead to the afterlife. The arrival of Christianity in Scandinavia shifted Old Norse cultures from an immediate to a transcendent religious model, altering their outlook on the afterlife. This transformation resulted in a hybrid version of the future, which Snorri Sturluson brilliantly captures in Gylfaginning.

This model provides several regions or Halls that one could visit after dying, some of which are shown as far more appealing than the traditional, depressing afterlife. However, to obtain these afterlives, a human had to live—or, more commonly, die—in a certain way.

Heathens today are free to construct their thoughts about death and the afterlife. Death notions are decentralized in Norse Heathenry because it is a decentralized religion.

NORSE HEATHENS ARE notorious for latching on to whichever idea best fits their values. Some people adopt a transcendental worldview in the hopes of reaching Valhalla or Fólkvangr. Others see Helheim as a pleasant and friendly Hall where they can reunite with their ancestors after death, comparable to the Old Norse underworld. Some belief in reincarnation and may or may not regard the Halls as transitory stopovers on their journey through life. On the other hand, others think people have the freedom to go wherever they want, irrespective of how they live and die.

Remember that the notion that existence must be conducted to indicate Heathen's heritage is a remnant of protestantism. Although not all Norse Pagans desire to visit Valhalla, they are no lesser Heathen for maintaining this belief.

4

OVERVIEW OF NORSE MYTHOLOGY

N obody can deny the significance of Norse Paganism even today, as it still has several followers all over the world. However, before understanding it in real letter and spirit, it is important to go through the Norse Mythology in detail. It comprises several concepts to gain all the much-needed insights about the topic.

Significance of Norse Mythology

Many people are familiar with religious characters as well as stories from the Norse clans who live in modern-day Scandinavia. On the other hand, Norse mythology is more than just a collection of fascinating people with extraordinary abilities.

NORSE MYTHOLOGY IS a part of the Germanic people groups of Europe's organized and old indigenous religion, which is practiced by communities in North and Central Europe who share similar language and religious customs. Before the Medieval Era, when Christianity had become the main religion, this religious belief was most prevalent.

BELIEVERS USED NORSE MYTHOLOGY STORIES, like any other religion's stories, to help organize and make sense of the world. The gods-breathing deities, a fundamental part of existence among the northwest Germanic peoples, were the protagonists in those myths.

Unlike many of today's major world faiths, the old Norse worshiped many gods, a religious faith in which many deities exist in mythology rather than a single god. Before their complete conversion to Christianity, the Germanic tribes worshiped 66 different gods and goddesses.

Odin had ascended to the throne of all gods by the Middle Ages. Scholars disagree over when this development took place, and there is a point to be made whether Tyr, a god of thunder, was initially the gods' leader. In any event, Odin was the heavenly household's head before the conversion of Germanic peoples to Christianity.

ODIN IS the partner of Freya, the mother goddess and beauty, but one of the most active gods. The Deity Loki charges Freya with engaging in sexual activity with all of the deities and the elves in one famous poetry. She disputes it, but Loki tells her that she had been discovered in her brother's arms. Freya is powerless to protect herself against this charge.

Below Odin, there were many more gods, some still well-known today. Thor, for instance, was a powerful god worshipped by all Germanic tribes. He was a devout warrior deity that carried a gigantic war hammer and could summon thunder. On the other hand, Loki was a shady trickster and the father of the half-giantess Hel, the underworld's ruler.

The distinction between Thor and Loki is crucial in understanding how Norse mythology's gods were viewed. The gods aren't supposed to be flawless or all-powerful. Instead, they portray real human characteristics, both good and negative.

AT FIRST, there was nothing but a vast emptiness. However, a zone of mist and frost expanded to the northwest of this gap, while an area of fire grew to the South. The North's name was Niflheim, while the South's was Muspellsheim; and the warmth from the latter dissolved some of the former's ice, forming Ymir, the Frost-Giant with such a physical figure. The species of Giants arose from Ymir's sweat, and as the glacier ice melted more, a massive calf was produced to feed the Monsters. This cow, in turn, was nourished by the salt in the ice. It licked the ice one day and hair appeared, then ahead, and Bur emerged fully formed the next day. Bur had three sons: Odin, Ve and Vili. Bur used to have a son, Buri, who already had 3 children: Odin, Vili, and Ve. These three belonged to a new race, gods rather than Giants. They banded together to assassinate Ymir. The majority of the other Titans perished in Ymir's blood, creating a massive sea. The three gods created solid ground, the Earth, from Ymir's body, and the dome of the heavens from Ymir's skull. Odin and his siblings subsequently used the larvae in Ymir's body to create the dwarven race. Other gods followed these three, and they built Asgard and all of its halls as their home.

After establishing their dominance, the gods created the first mortals, sculpting a man from such an elm tree and a female from such a vine. This first pair received breath, vitality, a soul, reasoning, warmth, and freshness from the gods. And Odin selected only the bravest of their male descendants to reside in Asgard after they perished, for these soldiers would aid him in the last battle against the forces of evil.

Yggdrasil, a massive ash tree, supported the cosmos. One of its branches reached out to Niflheim, the netherworld; one to Jötunheim, the realm of Giants; one more to Midgard, the kingdom of men; and yet another to Asgard, the kingdom of the gods. A squirrel and a hawk dwelt in its top branches, while the serpent Nidhögg lived at its rootage, gnawing away at the structure until it collapsed at the end of time. Meanwhile, the Dark elves, or Fates, kept the tree alive by watering it.

Odin understood that the gods' power was finite and that he and his companions would perish when the Titans and demons rose against them. The final battle will occur at Vigrid, a 100-mile-long and 100-mile-wide battlefield. Fenrir, the wolf, would consume Odin, but his child would avenge him. Thor and the Midgard Viper would kill each other, as would Loki and Heimdall, and Tyr would kill Garm, Niflheim's powerful hound, and then be clawed to death. As the world plunged beneath the waves, the stars and celestial beings would fall. The gods' twilight would turn tonight, and the world would cease to exist.

Despite this, there was still a force, the Nameless One, who would provide birth to a new planet beyond the horizon of time.

. . .

THE PRE-CHRISTIAN RELIGION, beliefs, and stories of the Scandinavian people, particularly those who lived in Iceland, where the literary works for Norse mythology were compiled, are known as Norse or Scandinavian mythology. (However, by using the phrase "Scandinavian," it's vital to remember that Finnish mythology is distinct from Norse mythology, despite certain parallels.) The finest form of the ancient common Germanic religion, which also contains the strongly linked Anglo-Saxon mythology, is Norse mythology. In turn, Germanic mythology evolved from older Indo-European mythology.

Norse mythology is a compilation of Northern Germanic tribes' shared beliefs and stories. It was not a revealed religion because it was not a truth passed down from the gods to mortals (though there are accounts of ordinary people hearing the tales of the deities from a trip to or from the deities). It did not have any text. Orally, the mythology was passed down in the form of extended, regular poetry. Oral transmission continued during the Viking Age, and we know a lot about it because of the Eddas and other medieval manuscripts written during and after Christianization.

THESE BELIEFS HAVE SURVIVED the longest in Scandinavian folklore, and some rural customs have survived today. Others, such as Germanic Neopaganism, have lately been revived or reinvented. Mythology has also been used as a source of inspiration in writing.

The world is depicted as a flat disc in Norse mythology. This disc is found among the Yggdrasil, or world tree, branches. Asgard, the gods' home, was in the circle's centre and could only be reached by crossing the rainbows. Jötun-heimr was the name of the Giants' home (giant realm).

Hel, Loki's daughter, ruled over Niflheim, a chilly, dark realm. The Prose Edda claimed that this was the final resting place for most of the dead. The burning land of Muspell, abode of the fire giants, was situated somewhere in the South.

Him, home of the light fairies (ljósálfar), Svartálfaheim, house of the dark elves, and Nidavellir, the homeland of the dwarves, are among the otherworldly regions. Midgard, the realm of mortals, lay midway between Asgard and Niflheim.

THE UNIVERSE of Norse mythology also includes a large component of duality: for example, night and day have myth-ical equivalents. This could have represented a more funda-mental philosophical faith in polarities as the world's foundation.

The worlds of ice Niflheim and fire Muspelheim existed initially, and behind them was the Ginnungagap, a "smiling (or yawning) gap" where nothing lived. The flame of Muspel-heim licked the ice in Ginnungagap, forming a primeval giant Ymir and a huge cow, Auumbla, whose milk nourished Ymir. The cow kissed the ice, giving birth to the first God, Bri, who was the parent of Borr, who was the parent of Odin and his sons Vili and Ve. Ymir was a transsexual who was the sole progenitor of the enormous race.

Borr's sons, Odin, Vili, and Ve, then slew Ymir and constructed the universe from his flesh. Odin, Vili, and Ve carved the dome of the sky from their skull, upheld by four dwarfs. They were given life by Odin, consciousness by Vili, and senses by Ve. Sol is the Deity of the Sun, Mundilfari's daughter, and Glen's wife. Every day, she flies over the sky in her chariot drawn by horses called Alsvid and Arvak. This section is called Alfrodull, which means "splendor of elves," a common name for the Sun. During the day, Sol is pursued by Skoll, a wolf who wants to consume her. Solar eclipses indicate that Skoll is closing in on her. Skoll will finally catch and consume Sol, but her daughter will succeed. Hati, another wolf, pursues Sol's brother, Mani.

Svalin, who dwells between both the Earth and Sol, protects this from the entire heat of the Sun. According to Norse religion, the Sun did not offer light but came from Arvak and Alsvid's manes.

THE FUTURE in Old Norse mythology is dismal. It was believed that the forces of disorder would eventually outweigh and defeat the human and divine defenders of order. The deceased will sail from Norse mythology to attack the living, with Loki and his monster progeny bursting their chains. With a blow on his horn, Heimdall, the gods' watchman, will call the heavenly host. After that, the gods will lose in a final fight between order and disorder (Ragnarök), as is his fate. Knowing this, the gods will collect the best soldiers, the Einherjar, to battle on their behalf when the time comes, but they will ultimately be powerless to stop the world from plunging into the chaos from which it once arose; the gods and their planet will be annihilated. Fenrir will swallow and consume.

. . .

YET, there are a few human and divine survivors who will inhabit a new world and restart the cycle. According to Sybil, a later addition to the tale betrays Christian influence; experts are split on whether this is a later development to the narrative that indicates Christian influence. The Völuspá's eschatology may represent an earlier Indo-European tradition linked to Persian Zoroastrianism's eschatology.

The Norse Chronology and Holidays: The Norse Cycle of the Year

Have you ever considered whether there is such a thing as "the Norse cycle of the year"? Or how did the Viking calendar look? As Vikings roamed and expanded over Europe, several calendars were discovered. Unfortunately, we do not have many documents about them, and those that have survived are largely Christian influenced.

Fortunately, these archaeological findings contained references to previous Pagan feasts. The old Icelandic timetable was utilized until the 18th century, so we may get a picture of how the ancient Germanic tribes structured their time using these materials.

UNLIKE OUR PRESENT GREGORIAN CALENDAR, the year was split into only two seasons: Summer and winter. The Vikings used the lunar phases to tell the time, from full moon through new moon, splitting the year into twelve months of thirty days and four additional days every fourth Summer termed the Sumarauki to compensate for leap years, despite the Sun's importance in their existence.

Solstices and equinoxes, like other civilizations, had considerable significance. These astronomical occurrences were extremely obvious in the northern parts and helped them estimate the coming of the various seasons, which was important for agriculture.

Norse Vacations

There are many distinct feasts and festivals on the Norse calendar, but we do not have complete records. Other of these celebrations were based on medieval manuscripts. In contrast, others were re-created using the limited information available from various sagas, with the Wiccan Cycle of the Year serving as inspiration in some cases.

Orrablot, or Husband's Day
It was observed in the first week of the month of Orri to honor all spouses and dads. It was conducted in honor of Thor and Thorri, the winter spirit.

Góublót, or Wife's Day
It was celebrated on the 1st day of Góa in commemoration of all mothers and spouses. It is also a time to mark the conclusion of the winter season.

Harpa's first day, Sigrblót
It is a day to commemorate the start of Summer and the triumph of sunlight over darkness. During the event, gifts to Freya were made.

On the 1st day of Winter, Alfarblót
It commemorates the end of the year's harvest and is linked to the goddess Freya. This festival was held in the

seclusion of each home rather than in the presence of others and was led by the ladies of the house.

Jól, or Yule

It is a northern European festival linked with the Great Hunt and Odin and the forerunner of modern Christmas celebrations.

Dsablót

This event's actual date is still unknown; some records claim it was held at the start of winter, while others claim it was held at the end; nonetheless, it might have been held on both days. The disir (female powers of guardianship and fertility), deities, ancestors, and other female figures from Norse mythology were also honored at this celebration.

Holidays of the Heathens

Steven Mcallen established the "Heathen Calendar" in 1975, drawing inspiration from the Wiccan Cycle of the Year and assigning Nordic titles to existing events in Northern Europe that Christianity highly impacted.

Midsummer (June 21st)

If you choose to celebrate on the real summer solstice, the date of the celebration may vary slightly. The brightest period of the year is celebrated with bonfires, traditional music, and the burning of maize dollies.

The Frey Feast

It is also known as Freysblot, takes place on August 1st and is a time of appreciation for the first crop of the year. As a gift to the God Frey, a bread loaf is cooked.

Fall Feast (September 23rd)

Because this festival happens on the Autumn equinox, the date may vary somewhat if observed on that day. It commemorates the season's second harvest and the beginning of the food-gathering season for the following winter months. It is also a moment to reflect on our accomplishments and be grateful for the gifts that the Earth has bestowed upon us.

Vetrnaetr (October 31st)

It signaled the end of the harvesting season, signaling that it was time to put the farm animals' meat to good use and begin hunting. It is also a day to remember and honor the goddess Hela and her ancestors. Because the veil between the realms is thinner on this night, it is also an ideal time to undertake some year-ahead divination.

Yule (20th December-1st January)

It is the most prominent Norse holiday, lasting 12 nights and beginning on December 20th. The darkest season of the year signals the start and end of all things and the closest approach of the divinities to Midgard. The dead come to Earth to feast with the alive, but other supernatural creatures are allowed to roam during this time.

History and Origin of Norse Mythology

The myths and stories of northeastern groups who spoke German gave rise to Norse mythology. It has a lot of similarities to pre-Christian Germanic mythology. Some of these groups brought their myths when they migrated to England and Scandinavia. Their traditional beliefs disappeared as they converted. However, Catholicism did not take root in Scandinavia until much later, and the Norse form of Germanic mythology flourished during the Viking era, which lasted roughly from 750 to 1050. Most Norse mythology is preserved in medieval writings, most of which have been authored in Iceland. Even after becoming Christians, generations of Norse colonists within this region were greatly interested in their heritage.

A book entitled the Poetic Edda, also called the Elder Edda, is a primary source of information on Norse mythology. It contains mythical and epic poems, notably Voluspa, a summary of Ancient mythology from creation to Ragnarok, the world's ultimate devastating war. The Poetic Edda was produced in Iceland circa 1270 by an unknown author who used texts dating from 800 to 1100.

Snorri Sturluson, an Icelandic writer and chieftain, composed the Prose Edda around 1222, which reinterpreted classic Icelandic poetry for modern audiences. A trip by Gylfi, a Swedish monarch, to Asgard, the home of the gods, was described in a section of the Prose Edda. The king interrogated the deities about their past exploitations and fate.

OTHER SCANDINAVIAN WRITINGS also contain Norse mythology. Many Norse poems allude to mythical persons or events. Icelanders began composing ancestral folk tales about their forefathers and heroic folk tales about their famous heroes in the early 1200s.

Many of these sagas included references to mythological figures and events. In the 1200s, Saxo Grammaticus, a Danish scholar, published a chronicle of the Danish people, which opened with a description of their pagan religions and ancient heroes. Germanic and Norse tales are also mentioned in the works of ancient Roman and medieval historians. Tacitus, a Roman historian, wrote Germania in AD 98, an account of the Germanic peoples that included some religious beliefs and rituals.

This faith was animistic (the belief that plants, animals, and inanimate objects had souls), polytheistic (worshipping numerous Gods), pantheistic (believing that the world is a representation of the deities), and held a cyclic view of time. Like many other early faiths, the mythology includes myths about the birth of the universe and humans and a supernatural explanation for day and darkness, weather, and natural phenomena.

The majority of the mythology we know now revolves around the gods' predicament and the stories surrounding their planet. Yggdrasil, the major cosmological tree in Norse mythology, is surrounded by nine worlds. All beings live in these nine circles:

- The Viking Gods live in the spiritual world of Asgard.
- Humanity lives in Midgard.
- Elves, giants, and dwarves live in the other worlds.

In myths and stories, travel between realms was widespread, and Gods, humans, and other beings would communicate directly.

Humanity was born from the blood of Ymir, an ancient entity, and the first two people were named Ask and Embla. After Ragnarok, the planet will be purportedly resurrected, a war between the Gods and their foes. The globe will be set ablaze and then reborn, fruitful and green, and two humans will again be able to repopulate the Earth.

Norse mythology is preserved in Old Norse dialects, a West Germanic language used in Europe throughout the Middle Ages. These texts were written down from oral history in manuscripts in Iceland during the thirteenth century. Poetry and Folk tales have provided the best insight into Norse beliefs and deities revered. Objects discovered in pagan burial sites, such as amulets with Thor's hammer and little female figures regarded as Valkyries, have depicted Norse mythology.

Historians agree that Thor was the most prominent Deity among the Vikings, based on evidence found in documents, place names, and manuscripts. Thor is shown as a courageous defender of humanity, wielding his hammer Mjolnir and destroying Jotnar, gods' and humanity's opponents. Loki is the mischievous God, also known as a disguise, accountable for the Gods' and humanity's conflict and turmoil. Odin is mentioned frequently in the extant literature, and he is shown as a one-eyed god with a wolf and raven flanking him as he seeks knowledge across the planets.

Odin hanged himself on Yggdrasil in a selfless gesture to learn the runic language, which he later gave to humanity. Odin is also the King of Valhalla, the Vikings' equivalent of heaven, and is thus frequently linked to death. Valhalla, a magnificent and massive hall in Asgard, was the afterlife for soldiers who died in battle, where they would fight all day and then spend their night dining, celebrating, and engaging in general debauchery. Warriors were held in great respect in Norse society.

Is Norse Magic a Thing?

Magic is allegedly limited to a ghetto of low-priced, semi paperback novels read by naive youths going through a rebellious phase in the modern world. "Magic," like "myth," is sometimes used as a disparaging term to describe barbarous superstitions that should be forgotten.

This should come as no surprise. Magic has no place in our contemporary, mechanistic worldview, which prefers to explain events primarily in terms of logical, predictable cause and effect relationships. Magic has been so thoroughly ejected from the world today – at least theoretically – that few people know what it is anymore. Most folks assume of magic as a kind of "god in the machine" that defies the "laws" that control matter and energy. After all, this is how magic is portrayed in mainstream cultures, such as those in the Harry Potter series. Understandably, folks whose only (mis)information about magic comes from modern culture would believe it to be what all these sources are telling them it is.

When one looks to other, more informed sources – as well as the Norse Eddas and folk tales are a good place to start – one discovers that magic is very different from what it is generally asserted to be these days. Also, inside the framework of some very different worldviews, magic is a wholly explained and even, in some ways, ordinary thing.

BY DEALING DIRECTLY WITH AWARENESS, magic brings about change. Its repercussions frequently cross over into the physical realm, but only inadvertently. This is the complete antithesis of what evolutionary theory does in many ways. According to the "laws" of the physical universe, science creates changes in the physical world. Magic and technology have different methods of operation, but they also have different goals, and this difference in goals explains the variance in methods. This is why scientists do not whisper chants before altars etched with emotionally evocative symbols and why magicians do not conduct laboratory studies. The defenders of modern customs frequently assert that magic is a "primitive," immature fumbling toward science and that magic is already outmoded because science has arrived.

On the other hand, science and magic are two quite distinct things. Neither can completely replace the other. Indeed, as we will see later, magic is as active and well as ever in the world today — it has just been ingeniously disguised.

The heathen Norse and other Germanic individuals thought that soul could be present in a wide variety of things all around the globe rather than being limited to humans. Even those we now perceive as nonliving, lifeless objects were included. And if it has a spirit, it is sentient and has a purpose of its own. As a result, humans were not the only ones who might be affected by magic. Because a storm, a cat, or a ship had spirit, they were all subject to the functioning of magic.

Magic was a somewhat common component of everyday life for the old Germanic peoples. Rather than working against the basic principles which were considered to underpin the functioning of the cosmos, magicians worked with them.

·   ·   ·

MODERN PEOPLE frequently distinguish between "white magic" and "black magic," with the former being "good" magic and the latter being "bad" magic. This is just as prevalent in the anthropological domain as in the general public. On the other hand, such a classification is absent from pre-Christian Germanic peoples' notions of magic, who had widely divergent moral standards than what we now call "morality."

The Modern World's Magic

Until the Renaissance, magic was an important component of the Western world. However, the dreadfully pious and reactionary aspects of European society in the 16th and 17th centuries crushed the "Rebirth" of Classical civilization, arts, and sciences, which included the Protestant Reformation, the Catholic Response, the Inquisition, as well as the Witch Trials. Philosophers and scientists, who were previously among the most likely to be passionate practitioners of magic, scrubbed their crafts about anything that might appear "magical," branding it as the investigation of inert, mechanistic phenomena, out of obvious concern for their safety. This aligned their disciplines with the prevalent Christian theological strains, which hold that the observable, tangible universe is a thoughtless, unfeeling item made by a god entirely distinct from his creation. Fortunately, consciousness was banished again from the world from the human brain, which was reframed in mechanical rather than animistic terms. Magic had been banned from the globe - solely for ideological reasons.

The Norse faiths practiced before science and computational technology suit the criteria of Pagan, as we can see from the definitions. Reading it back via epics, historic chronicles, mythology, and the unusual rant of a Frankish priest, it is evident that the Vikings practiced not just a method of worship but also a code of morals that was incomparably different from our "modern" standardized faiths.

The majority of citizens were conscious that the Norse and Scandinavian communities were polytheistic (they believed in multiple gods). Still, few were aware of the specific link between the Norse gods and the people. There was a cause why the Vikings not just trusted in magic but also considered it essential in their daily lives. This was owing to the strange interactions the Vikings had with their various gods.

THANKS TO MARVEL'S film series featuring a Hollywood hunk as Thor, the Norse Deity who wields the huge hammer Mjolnir, many people are familiar with Thor, Odin, Loki and Freya.

The gods of Norse mythology were not kind. They did not despise man; in fact, the reverse was true. The gods loved humanity, but not as much as Zeus. That guy was obsessed with everything, like there was nothing he could not get pregnant with. The Norse gods liked humans, but they did not feel compelled to contact them. Humans and gods existed on separate planes of existence — chronological and everlasting – and each would have its issues. And it was due for such a reason that the Vikings required magic.

Everything was under the supervision of the gods, not in a dictating sense. The gods were nothing more than embodiments of forces of nature and qualities of being. There would have been no elegance in the universe if Freya did not exist; there would have been no poetry if Braggi did not exist, and so on.

5

NORSE MAGIC FOR BEGINNERS

N orse Magic holds a special place in the religion of Norse Paganism. The concepts of magic and runes concerning paganism can be found in several ancient as well as modern-age books. However, understating it in the real sense of the word will require you to go through the key terms and basic concepts in detail. This chapter will take you through such explanations in detail.

Norse Magic and Runes

Runic inscriptions were said to have magical properties in the sagas. You may use inscriptions to foresee the future, protect someone from bad luck, endow objects with various traits, or note down conjurations, spells, and curses. The majority of runic inscriptions discovered so far, on the other hand, convey more mundane statements. These have been cut to be used regularly.

We learn about how runes and magic words were

employed concerning the health of the sagas. The skald Egil used lines to cure a little girl whose false runes had bewitched in Egil Skallagrimsson's story. Egil managed to carve new runes and set them under the girl's pillow, healing her. The narrative concludes that in the wrong hands, runes, as well as words, can be dangerous.

Runes engraved on runestones performed a variety of functions as well. The writing on the Glavendrup stone in Funen, for example, included a caution to anyone who would destroy or transport the stone.

Ragnhildr erected this stone in remembrance of Alli the Pale, sanctuary priest and honorable egn of the entourage, according to the runic inscription. Alli's kids built the memorial to remember their father and by his widow in remembrance of her husband. In honour of his lord, Sóti engraved these runes. He who damaged this rock or pulled it (to stand) in remembrance of another was a warlock. This final phrase imposes a curse on anyone who broke the stone or used it to memorialize someone else.

IN DENMARK, runes were engraved during the medieval period as well as during the Viking Age. A large number of medieval runic writings have been discovered in recent years. These inscriptions were carved for various reasons, including honoring God, serious goals, and amusement.

Runic magic was not lost, and curses inscribed in runes could be seen on medieval staffs. The wielder of the runic staff and wands waved it towards the person they desired to "capture." According to medieval songs, runes might be used to charm a woman. Stig is in love with Kirsten in the ballad

"The Knight Stig's runes and wedding." With the help of a rune staff, he tries to capture her love. However, the staff rolls under Princess Regitze's dress, causing the enchantment to work on her instead. Stig is forced to marry the princess since she finds love with him soon.

The runic inscriptions from the Middle Ages have been evidence of the Danes' adherence to their prior beliefs. However, numerous inscriptions are linked to Christianity. Runic inscriptions can be found on thurials, church bells, and amulets. Some may have thought such inscriptions were rudimentary during medieval times. They were, nevertheless, most likely an efficient form of communication with the congregation's Latin-illiterate members.

In Norse Paganism, the runes have significant spiritual importance. Odin is claimed to have discovered the mysteries of runic language after hanging himself on the cosmic tree Yggdrasil for 9 days and nights, impaled with a spear—self-sacrifice. For this reason, they are frequently found in Norse Pagan practice.

Historically, the runes were employed for both practical and magical purposes. The Norse used their writing for memorial messages on artifacts like tools and runestones rather than extended writings like books. To enchant objects, charms were also written on them. However, the method by which these charms were made remained unknown. There is no instruction manual for making them, and we can't determine how they were constructed merely by glancing at them.

The runes were utilized for Runic Calendars until the twentieth century after the Reformation of Scandinavia, which concluded around 1100 CE. Futhark characters were associated with numerals in these calendars, marking key days of the year, such as spring equinox, equinoxes, and feast.

Bind runes are cords formed by joining two or more runes together. Their historical purpose was primarily aesthetic, comparable to how curly braces are employed today to make particular letters look nicer when stacked together.

IN CURRENT USAGE, "BINDRUNES" refers to a magical signalization system. Making a bindrune entails creating a monogram made of runes with meanings that suit the bindrune's intended usage. This type of magic is quite new, and it is extremely close to the civilization approach created by Austin Osman Spare for Chaos Magic.

RUNES WERE NOT MEANT to be used every day. The Northmen's past was conveyed orally, with runes only being used to record significant events. Let's explore the incredible storyline of the Viking language in depth.

Viking runes have a long and illustrious history. The basis of the runes used by Germanic peoples of Mainland Europe in the first century of the Eighth Century is a point of contention. The characters are similar to those in other writing systems, and none of them has matched up perfectly enough for the scholars to say, "Yep, this is it."

THE RUNES ARE DESCENDED from ancient Italic writings seen on the Italian peninsula, derived from the Greek script.

They probably originated from the Etruscan language, which evolved into the Latin script from English and most Western languages today.

THE PHRASE 'RUNIC ALPHABETS' is frequently used to describe the rune systems, and it is a perfectly appropriate term for most people.

However, the letters' alpha beta' and 'aleph beth' are the first two letters of the Greek and Hebrew alphabets, respectively. The runes begin with F and U rather than A and B, which might lead to some intriguing complications!

INSTEAD, after the first six letters: F, U, Th/, A, R, and K, researchers point to the Nordic runic scripts as a Futhark or Fuark. If you have ever questioned where the letter thorn originates from, it's because of the runes.

The word rune is taken from the German root run, which means "secret" or "whisper." The term has similar implications in the Celtic language, yet it can also refer to knife cutting, speaking, or a miracle. Because runes were devised by and known exclusively to the elite, in the beginning, the word might refer to 'secrets.'

The magical aspect of runes is frequently mentioned, yet empirical evidence rarely supports it. How much we do understand is that runic markings were often used to commemorate significant events or people. This was not your typical alphabet in the Viking Age.

The Significance of Runes

We have a solid grasp of the runes and how they are translated into modern characters. It is harder to figure out what they were trying to say.

BECAUSE THE YOUNGER Futhark is so tiny, each character can represent a variety of sounds. If you don't know the context, it is difficult to discern which of the noises was intended. For example, the I rune was employed to represent the characters, e and I, so a word like "pick" might mean "pick" or "peck."

Another difficulty is that runes were frequently repurposed for new sounds as the language progressed away from specific sounds or towards others, making them outdated. As a result, KAT might stand for cat, depending on when it was written and whether the author was updated on new sounds.

The background of some runestones is obvious, and the meaning is straightforward. We will never know exactly what others are saying, and the best we can do is guess.

The Present-Day Application Runes of the Vikings

The fact that the far-right, especially neo-nazis, have taken many of the runes is a sobering reality. The most noteworthy is the Sowilo rune, which also functioned as the SS's symbol. Algiz, AEihwaz, Hagal and Othala all have different connotations in Nazi Germany. The Armanen runes were created by Guido von List using lines from the Younger Futhark.

These signs are now worn as inconspicuous signs of affection for far-right and neo-nazi ideology as necklaces or piercings that do not draw attention to themselves. A Swastika is identifiable, but only those well-versed in the subject can understand the meaning of a sigil like the Othala.

Role-players and Viking or runic lovers are battling these organizations to reclaim the markings. They want to be able to wear and use runes without fear of the negative connotations.

The Bluetooth logo, which may be found on thousands of electronic devices worldwide, combines the hagall and bjarkan runes. The names of Harald Bltan, sometimes known as Harald Gormsson, as well as renowned by the nickname Bluetooth, are referenced in these letters. Harald was a Norse king who ruled over Europe during the Viking Age.

IN NORSE MYTHOLOGY, the deity Odin pierced his heart with his sword and hung for nine nights and days on the globe tree Yggdrasil to understand the runes. The Norns were using the runes to carry destiny up the trunk and branch offices of Yggdrasil towards the 9 worlds in amongst its boughs. Odin committed his sacrifice in severe pain and at great risk to himself when he knew the runes had significant meaning and that if he could decipher them, he would acquire profound understanding and power.

Since the first century, the Norse and other Germanic peoples have used runes to write. However, they did not use this writing in the same manner that we do now, nor did they use it in the same way that the Mediterranean and other nearby cultures did at the time. Instead, runes were used for important inscriptions. They might be engraved into rune rocks to honour ancestors and remember heroes' tombs. They might be employed as spells for safety or success because they had purpose or meaning. Hence, they can be used to communicate between natural and supernatural worlds. Many of these runes, like the T, O, F, and S visible in these pendants, are apparent influences on today's modern English letters.

They might be cast and interpreted to detect the present or forecast the future if they were engraved on a stick. Runes were frequently engraved on wood, bones, or stone rather than written on parchment or canvas, which explains their angular shape. While evidence reveals that most Vikings could read the runes on a basic level, actual study and comprehension of these signs was a godly quest for them.

The runes have their beginnings in the times when German warbands attacked people who lived south of themselves in what is now Italy. Scholars disagree over whether the runes came from an Old Italian alphabet or an Etruscan script. The Germanic warbands might have carried back the alphabet from their raids to the South.

Runes have magical capabilities in addition to their being used as written code. For protection and healing, runes were frequently utilized in magical charms. They might also be utilized to cast a spell. Runes were supposed to have magical properties.

How to Make Your Runes?

Although you can buy pre-made runes, many Norse magic practitioners believe making your runes is a tradition. It is not necessarily required, but it may be optimum in a magical sense for some people. According to Tacitus' Germania, the Runes should be constructed from any nut-bearing tree, including oak, hazel, and possibly pines or cedars.

Staining runes red to depict blood is also a common method in rune-making. The runes are questioned, according to Tacitus, by casting them upon a white linen sheet and lifting them while maintaining one's gaze fixed on the skies above.

Like other kinds of divination, someone reading runes will usually focus on a specific situation and consider past and present influences. They also consider what would happen if one continued on their current route. Individual choices can affect the future. The rune caster can assist the querent in considering possible outcomes by thinking about cause and effect.

However, it is crucial to note that carving is an important aspect of the magic for those who work with runes, and it should not be treated lightly or even without preparation and expertise.

How to Make a Rune Set from Scratch?

Are you interested in getting information about astrology? Then rune cast is indeed a fantastic place to begin! Although mastering them can take years, you can quickly construct your rune set & learn the fundamental concepts.

There are other runic alphabetic characters, but the Elder Futhark, which consists of 24 letters, is the most commonly used for rune divination. An empty rune known as Wyrd rune or Odin's rune is included in some rune sets. However, this is a more recent inclusion with no documentary records of its existence.

If you are unaware of the rune casting procedure, you might be wondering if you can make your runes. Should you make your own or buy a prepared set?

Purchasing a rune set is easy, and there is perfectly nothing bad with it, so do not be scared to do so if you find one that appeals to you. They are frequently made of difficult-to-find materials, such as metal, crystals or glass.

On the other hand, creating your rune set will help you feel linked to it because it will contain your power and unique touch. It is also a cost-effective way to get started if you are unsure if divination is right for you.

Spell Jars for Beginners

Norse mythology mostly depends on the Eddas and other medieval literature written down during and after Christianization. Our understanding primarily depends on what was orally conveyed in the poetry. These texts are made up of tales and beliefs shared by Northeast Germanic tribes.

Norse, Viking, or Scandinavian mythology is the foundation of the Scandinavian peoples' original pre-Christian religion, beliefs, and tales.

NORSE PAGANISM INCLUDES pre-indigenous religious notions shared by the Northern Germanic tribes. As a result, Norse religion is a subgroup of Germanic religion, which was practiced till the end of the Viking Age across the territories inhabited by Germanic tribes over most of Central and Northern Europe.

Völva - Norse Paganism's Wise Women
In Norse & Germanic paganism, Völva was indeed a wise

woman, healer, or priestess. They were highly regarded members of society who used herbalism and prophesy to care for their people's spiritual and bodily needs. Some argue that with the arrival of Christianity, Völva became marginalized and persecuted, and they would linger on in the northern European idea of the witch. They frequently appear in Norse mythology.

Shamanism, sorcery, prophesy, and other kinds of indigenous magic were all practiced by völva. Völvas were thought to have such abilities in mythological depictions that even the gods' father, Odin, consulted a völva to see what the gods' future contained.

ACCORDING TO EARLY REPORTS, they were elderly white women who sacrificed prisoners of battle and splashed their blood. It was thought that they could predict the future by doing so.

Seidr

Seidr is an old Norse name before Norsemen and women who practiced sorcery or witchcraft. Spell invocation, galdrar (deceitful magic), and divination were all part of Seidr, mostly practiced by women (Völva). Some men performed seidr as well, and they were not regarded in the same regard as the ladies.

Seidr was practiced by Freya and other deities of Norse mythology. Odin also practiced it, whom Loki had mocked for just doing that because it was deemed unmanly. Freya taught Odin the skill of seidr.

Freya, Goddess of Magic and Sex

Freya is the mother goddess of love, elegance, sex, attraction, fertility, crops, birth in Norse mythology, and the ultimate emblem of sensuality. She was a deity of war, mortality, magic, predictions, and wealth and was the most attractive of the goddesses. She adores music, spring, and flowers, and she has a special fondness for fairies. Freya is among the Vanir's most important goddesses; her name means "lady" in Old Norse.

THE VANIR IS a collection of wild places and reproduction gods and goddesses in Norse mythology who are sworn adversaries of the Aesir warrior gods. They were thought to be masters of magic and bringers of health, beauty, fertility, luck, and money. Vanaheim is the home of the Vanir.

She is indeed the sister of Freyr and the child of the Deity Njord. She then married the enigmatic God Od (perhaps another incarnation of Odin), who then vanished. Her tears turned to gold as she mourned the loss of her husband.

Freya is represented as riding in a chariot drawn by two cats and carrying a garment (or skin) made of bird feathers that permits her to transform into a falcon. Hildesvini ("battle boar"), her human boyfriend Ottar in disguise, is her property. Fulla is her chambermaid. Freya resides in the lovely palace Folkvang ("field of people"), which is always filled with love music, and her chamber is Sessrumnir. With Odin, she separates the slain soldiers into two groups: one travels to her palace, and the other goes to Valhalla. Women also visit her hall.

Pagans refer to all Earth-based polytheistic traditions for those unfamiliar with this faith. It comprises Asatru, Wicca,

Druidism, Slavic Paganism, Roman and Egyptian Paganism, and many others, all of which have a common theme of worshipping nature and numerous deities. Witchcraft is a spiritual discipline or craft that honors nature and relies on intention, belief, and ritual activities to bring about positive change in one's life.

Magic and Paganism

Regis Boyer, a French Viking researcher, picked the term Le monde du dual, 'the universe of the double,' for his study on Old Norse magic, which he published in 1986. As he points out in his introduction, it is frequently surprising to realize how important magic was in the Nordic mental realm. He tries to depict this as a type of alternative belief, a glass held up beside the more exalted apparatus of Viking religion, in his notion of the 'Double.'

We have already been shown how current notions of "religion" are not always consistent with the Middle Ages. Similarly, we can draw a similar remark regarding the social milieu of sorcery. The initial issues arise at the basis of what appears to be a basic definition, but which, upon closer recognition, are revealed to be less than simple. Today, we interchangeably refer to 'magic' and 'witchcraft,' and the casting of 'spells' and 'charms,' all carried out by 'sorcerers,' 'witches,' 'warlocks,' and 'wizards,' among others. There is no difference between certain names in everyday speech, yet no one would associate them with institutional faith as it is often understood. The situation was considerably different in the early medieval period in two ways.

To begin with, there appears to have been a fairly specific

lexicon of sorcery, which included its forms, functions, practices, and practitioners. Second, the entire system of sorcery was intertwined with that of worship through personal connections with gods and goddesses. It also included Finn and Freyja and its basic principles, which incorporated a few of the spiritual beliefs discussed above.

When stated in this manner, it is obvious from literary sources that the concept stood above all others at the heart of Old Norse's magical concepts.

SEIDR WOULD ALSO HAVE BEEN SPOKEN ROUGHLY 'say the' rhyming with modern English' swathe,' but in the genitive form with a somewhat inflected 'r' note at the end (akin to 'the' being spoken before a vowel, thus 'rather'). Several researchers have remarked that it appears etymologically related to a collection of Indian strategic words with 'binding' implications, particularly in a ritualist's context.

It is explained in detail in various Old Norse writings and inferentially in a large number of others. All of these are discussed in further depth below, but for now, suffice it to say that it appears to be unified for a huge number of acts, each of which served a particular purpose inside the bigger structure of sorcery. There were seidr ceremonies for divination and prophecy, as well as for healing the ill, bringing good luck, manipulating the weather, and calling game animals and fish. It may also be employed for the antithesis of these things: to condemn a person or an organization; to ruin the land to make it unproductive; to cause illness; to predict false destinies. Ultimately, it leads the recipients on a path to disaster, harm, maiming, and murder, especially in family disturbances and battles.

. . .

SEIDR APPEARS TO HAVE BEEN, more than anything, an expansion of the intellect and its faculties. It generally involved clouding judgment, freezing of the will, and fatal hesitation, rather than direct violence, even on the battlefield. It was also tied to the calling of various entities and other beings who might be tied to the magician's will and sent forth to perform her or his will. A significant group of these beings, similar to the 'invisible population,' were extensions of the person in the expressions of a double spirit - the Jylgjur, hamingjur, etc.

In various sources, the Deity OSinnis described as the ultimate master of seidr, together with Freyja, from whom he learned its power. In their function as gods and goddesses of fertility and reproductive potency, the Vanir hint at another crucial facet of this sorcery. Many seidr rituals appear to be sexual in their goals and how they were performed. This focus on sexuality can be observed in many seidr's various roles reviewed above and activities with specific carnal goals. As a result, the execution of these rites appears to have placed such a high demand on their actors that they were marked with a separate type of gender identification outside of Viking Age society's conventions.

As a result of all of these factors, seidr has long been seen as a Norse parallel to what is often referred to as shamanism. The following chapters are devoted to this and the situational relations and functions of seidr. We will focus on seidr's use in war and as an element of what may be described as a divinely-inspired philosophy of martial heroism, backed up by the sexual and gender constructions that supported it. Nevertheless, seidr is hardly the only type of sorcery recorded in the Old Norse traditions. We must first explore these other spellcasters, their relationship to seidr, and how they may be viewed collectively before moving on.

Galdr, which appears to have been a specialized form of sorcery concentrating on a certain high-pitched singing style, is undoubtedly the most peculiar of these five. The current Swedish verb gala, which is used to describe the gloating of a hen and the most penetrating of birdcalls, is related to the word. The saga accounts of galdr-songs mention that they were good to the ears, and there is a notion of a specific rhythm in light of Snorri's description of galdralag in Hdttatal, which is utilized sometimes in Eddie poems like Hdvamdl and Sigrdrifomdl.

War Lindquist published one of the first important studies of the type, but he used the term quite loosely to refer to a variety of wonders from the Iron Age. Galdr was most commonly used for cursing, according to Reichborn-Kjen-nerud, who emphasizes the devastating capabilities of the tongue, citing an example of its use to cause various illnesses in both people and animals, as well as to kill. He claims that galdr and ancient runes lore have a strong relationship.

IT PERFORMED many of the same roles as seidr, if not all, and the two are frequently used together. Despite this, the seidr is always the one who establishes the overall pattern for the ceremony.

Galdr is better understood as a component of a larger system of operative magical activity, a tool in the ritual toolbox. The phrase was becoming synonymous with magic in general by the Middle Ages. Gandr is yet another unique group in this list, with origins that predate the Viking Age. The word's basic meaning is frequently considered to be 'magic,' and de Vries also stated that it is tied to the idea of Ginnungagap. This is significant because it implies that gandr was one of the funda- mental interactions from which the worlds were created, and hence that sort of ritualist power was of great importance.

The name Ganna, assigned by Dio Cassius in the Clas- sical History to the high priestess of both the German Semnones and derived from the same root, shows that this sort of sorcery had an early history.

We discover combinations of ceremonial forms by the Middle Ages, just as we do with galdr. There are allusions to sorceresses employing gandr in combination with seidr to prophecy in many places. In the notion of spiritual beings and the group that might be used to summon them, the phrase had a particular meaning.

Another part of Norse witchcraft was the practice of oiutiseta, or 'sitting out,' which appeared to have been more of a tactic for putting other procedures into effect than a specific ritual. It appeared to have entailed sitting out there at night, in particular settings such as burial sites, alongside running water, or under the corpses of the hanged, to obtain spiritual strength.

Beyond the specialized complexes of galdr and seidr, which the Deity employs, OSinn's rites form a genre of their own. Some of them are also accessible to human wizards. Still, Eddie's poetry makes it apparent that they are among the powers acquired by the Deity during his numerous travels for magical knowledge. These abilities are documented in the lists of spells in poems like Havamal, in runes of power catalogs, and saga narratives.

We now find another subcategory of 'general' sorcery, in addition to OSinn's magic. One part of this is a vocabulary of phrases that appears to simply mean 'magic' in the same hazy sense in which we use the term today. The most popular of them is -wasjjglkyngi, which appears to have been widely utilized. Throughout the Middle Ages, the latter idea grew in popularity, and it, along with galdr, remained one of the generic terms for 'witchcraft' well into post-medieval times.

Other terms that were identified as communes were also used. These include chants like gerningar, Ijod, and taufr and the complexity of runic lore as laid down in Eddie's poems like Sigrdrifomdl and Rigspula. Another set of phrases alludes to various sorts of unidentified magical knowledge and affixes denoting those individuals or supernatural beings who possess it. As a result, we find visenda-, kunatta-, and similar words meaning 'those who know,' a widespread notion of ritualist power in many cultures.

To what extent can we explain Old Norse magic in general terms, and can we employ seidr terminology for this purpose, given these 'other' magics?

The answer lies in the concept of magic itself, in both broad senses used by religious historians and in the context of the Viking Age. Without the above-mentioned 'worship' conventions, humans' relationship with the gods was not equal. All of the various types of cult activity we have looked at unavoidably entailed a degree of subservience.

· · ·

THIS IS ESPECIALLY true of the concept of blot, or 'sacrifice.' That is not the case in the magic domain, which is based on the concept of control. Humans appear to have used magic to actively direct the acts of mythical entities for their objectives, luring or summoning them first and then tying them to do the dragon's will.

This concept appears in one way or another in all of the magic discussions mentioned above, although only one of them - seidr - expresses it explicitly. This 'binding' magic is the only one in the ancient texts conceived as a full sort of magic and the only one that integrates components of the others into a bigger whole. Although both gandr and galdr are classified in recorded sources, the first was more like a technique, whereas the latter referred to a general type of sorcerous force from which all strength was derived.

IN THIS SENSE, there is justification for considering seidr as a common term for Old Norse magic. However, the overall ambiguity of portrayals of Viking magic justifies that the absence of consistent orthodoxy was an inherent component of the Norse approach toward the spiritual. We have seemed to find seidr used both as a precise and as a generalization for 'sorcery' throughout our contemporary understanding of the word in the sources. We appear to be following the pattern in which the Norse originally understood the concept by utilizing seidr as a major potential source that implicitly encompasses the other magics.

6

NORSE PAGANISM TODAY

The Asatru Association is an Icelandic religious formalized organization of Heathenry established on the First Day of Summer in 1972 by Sveinbjörn Beinteinsson, a farmer and poet. The First Day of Summer in Iceland is a national holiday and is celebrated on the first Thursday after April 18th annually. The Asatru Association was recognized and registered as a religious organization in 1973. The chief religious official or the highest office of the Asatru Association is referred to as "Allsherjargodi," an elected post.

THE PRIESTS in Asatru are called Godi, and each Godi is given a congregation called godord to work with. While each godord is more or less connected to certain geographic regions, there is no compulsion to join any specific godord. You are free to join any congregation that you like.

. . .

THE LEGAL APPROVAL allowed the organization to conduct legally binding rituals and ceremonies as well as to collect a share of the church tax, which is imposed by the tax on religious congregations to run and manage churches and their employees. Sveinbjörn Beinteinsson led this organization from its inception in 1972 until he died in 1993. During his time, the membership of this organization did not exceed 100 people, and there was not much activity.

THE SECOND ALLSHERJARGODI was Jörmundur Ingi Hansen, who led the organization from 1994 to 2002, and it was during this time that the Asatru Association witnessed considerable activity and growth. The third and current leader is the musician Hilmar Örn Hilmarsson, who took charge in 2003.

ASATRU DOES NOT CONFORM to a fixed religion, theology, or dogma. Each individual is free to have his or her own beliefs. For example, many Wiccan members are also members of the Asatru Association. The Asatru priests believe in a pantheistic perspective. The communal blot feast is the central ritual of Asatru. The priests also conduct naming ceremonies called gooar, weddings, funerals, coming of age, and other rituals too.

THE WORLDWIDE MAP of Heathens is a great way to connect with other Heathens too. Here is a step-by-step of how you use this map. The website link is given later on.

OPEN the map from the link and zoom in to your area. Even if you don't find anyone very close to your home, you will likely find Heathens within driving distance of your place of residence.

MOREOVER, even if you don't find anyone close to where you live, you can contact many believers (even if they live far away). They are likely to connect you with someone they know who, perhaps, lives closer to you.

DON'T FORGET to add yourself to the map. Someone in the future might find you and seek out your guidance. This is your way of making the path of Heathenry smoother for new entrants.

IF YOU WANT SOMETHING BADLY, the universe will find a way to bring it to you. Therefore, keep your desire to become an Asatru burning through self-learning and self-development. The more you delve deeper into yourself, the more your knowledge about the external world expands. Continue your efforts to connect with fellow believers. Sooner rather than later, you are likely to meet with such people and have a great community to rely on.

Norse Paganism in the Modern World

According to the Asatruars, Asatru is a revival of the ancient Norse Paganism beliefs. The word "revival" is key to fully understanding the nature of this religion in the modern world. Following the Christianization of Northern Europe, all that was left of Norse Paganism was the small number of people who could covertly practice their beliefs without getting found out. The religion had almost died out by the

12th Century. In the late 20th Century, some decided to rekindle the flame, choosing to reconnect with their ancestors' pre-Christian beliefs. In other words, Norse Paganism is not a modern creation but a revival of a religion that existed for centuries before.

AN ASATRUAR'S most distinguishing feature is their connection to themselves, their people, and nature. Most Asatruars have deep connections with their respective universes because they were taught to open up and embrace their spirituality. Since heathens are taught to see themselves as powerful beings equal to the Norse gods, they gradually gain the confidence needed to navigate their path in life.

GIVEN the lack of a fixed dogma and the fact that many new believers converted to Norse Paganism from monotheistic religions, there are many interpretations of the Pagan texts and various understandings of several topics, such as how the gods interact with humans and whether or not the Vaettir are considered gods. With all of the differences, there is a sense of mutual respect and understanding of different points of view and interpretations. Asatru priests, on the other hand, are not believed to be inherently better than any other practitioner but rather as people who have a strong devotion to their religion.

THE ORIGIN of Asatru is a fascinating story. It is almost unbelievable that this religion can survive centuries of Christianization behind hidden doors and then make its way out into the modern world centuries later. This only emphasizes the significance and weight of the connection between Norse

Paganism and Norse identity. Asatru would not have emerged if there had not been a strong desire among modern peoples to reconnect with nature and their ancestors' beliefs. The only thing more intriguing is how religion has evolved to adapt to modern times. It is not only interesting from an academic standpoint, but it also demonstrates that Norse Paganism is an ever-changing set of concepts and beliefs, and therefore a living, breathing religion.

ASATRU IS BASED on Snorri Sturluson's Poetic and Prose Eddas, which were written in the 13th century. However, in contrast to systemic religions, there is no single indisputable source or concrete interpretation. Using the Eddas (texts and individual/group interpretations), folklore, and information passed down from generation to generation, believers have reconstructed Norse Paganism in the most authentic way possible. While some elements, such as blood sacrifices and tribe protection, have been modernized as humans have evolved socially, economically, and morally, the core intention behind all rituals and concepts has not evolved. The revival process was and is the delicate process of deconstructing and analyzing the Eddas in search for what lies at the center of the ancient Norse Pagans' beliefs and relationship with their Gods and spirits and their universe altogether.

Where to Find Fellow Believers

Here are some suggestions and recommendations you can use to find fellow-Asatruars in your local community or the area you live in.

.   .   .

THE ASATRU FOLK ASSEMBLY is a global organization with branches and representatives found in many parts of the world. You can visit their website **https://www. runestone.org/** for more information. In addition to helping you in your research about Asatru and its customs and traditions, you can also go to their "Folkbuilder" page and connect with a team member. They, in turn, can help you find someone closer to where you live.

ANOTHER ASATRU COMMUNITY with a presence on the Internet is The Troth **https://thetroth.org/**. You can register yourself there if you wish. Scout under the "Find your local troth representative," and you are likely to discover an individual or group closer to your place of residence.

GET in touch with the kindred in the cities closest to you and connect with them. Most of these people will have some idea of how to help you build your heathen connection. Here are a few tips to help you get started:

- Do an Internet search with the words "Asatru/kindred/Heathen, [your city name]" using different search engines. You are likely to get some results from such searches, including names, contact numbers, and addresses. You can begin with this basic information.
- Use social media platforms to find Asatru connections. Many kindred groups have a dedicated page on most of the popular social media platforms.
- You can set up a local meet group using one of the paid apps that connect with other believers.

Although you might have to spend money, it could be worth your efforts. Still, you need to use this only if the earlier attempts don't work.

- Another way of contacting Heathens is to get in touch with other Pagan believers in your area, such as Wiccans. Considering that many Heathens start their Asatru journey from Wiccan beliefs, these connections are likely to help you get in touch with practicing Asatruars.

Temples

Manheim opened in Denmark in 2016 and was the first pagan temple in the country since the Middle Ages.

OTHER MODERN PAGAN TEMPLES CURRENTLY OPERATING ARE THE ÁSAHEIMUR HOF, in Efri Ás, Skagafjörður, and the Arctic Henge (Heimskautsgerðið), in Raufarhöfn in Iceland. The Odinist Fellowship Temple, in Newark-On-Trent in the United Kingdom, the Baldurshof, Asatru Folk Assembly temple, in Murdock, Minnesota, the New Grange Hall Ásatrú Hof, in Brownsville, Yuba County, California, and the Thorshof, Asatru Folk Assembly temple, in Linden, North Carolina, in the United States.

APART FROM THOSE, there are two temples under construction, one in the United States and one in Iceland.

. . .

THE FIRST IS the Atlanta Heathen Hof, which will be a temple for the group Vör Fórn Siðr. It is 10 miles outside Atlanta, Georgia, and will hopefully be fully completed by 2022.

THE SECOND ONE IS IN REYKJAVIK, Iceland. The Hof Ásatrúar-félagsins is under construction by the Ásatrúarfélagið and is currently being built in stages as it has been delayed several times.

HERE IS a small list of kindred you can connect to, learn from, or contact to find your fellow Heathens. You can send them an email and ask for their contact details or pose your questions:

NORTHERN MIST KINDRED – Located in Oakland County in Southern Michigan, the Northern Mist Kindred is a large group of Pagans with followers from different branches of Paganism. This group is focused on improving their knowledge and wisdom about Paganism and its varied belief systems.

KENAZ KINDRED – This group follows and worships the pantheon of Nordic gods and goddesses and focuses on the conservation of our planet and nature. They accept people from all cultural and racial backgrounds into their fold because they believe everyone has the right to worship and follow Norse Paganism and its gods and deities. They believe in the Nine Noble Virtues of the Odinic Rite. They are located in Eugene, Oregon.

.   .   .

SHIELDWALL KINDRED – Based out of Utah, this small Asatru group's primary aim is to expand their membership, gain knowledge and wisdom, and share it with people who don't know about Heathenism and its authentic nature. This group believes strongly in the Aesir and Vanir gods, and they respect the influence these gods have on Midgard and its people.

PEOPLE from all races and communities are welcomed into this group, and they do not restrict entry only to people of Germanic origin. According to their belief, their gods and goddesses traveled all over the world, and therefore, everyone should be allowed into the Asatru fold. This group is dedicated to helping new Heathens build their knowledge about Heathenism so that they can imbibe Asatru values and principles into their lives and expand their mental, physical, and spiritual capabilities.

NORTHERN PINES HEATHEN KINDRED – Located in Northern Ontario, this Heathen kindred believes in self-preservation and self-sustenance. They honor and maintain a deep connection with their ancestors and the Asatru community. They believe in following the kindred honor code strictly along with the Nine Noble Virtues.

THEY FOLLOW and celebrate the traditional Asatru feasts and festivals, organizing rituals, ceremonies, and celebrations according to each festival. They believe in and follow the Asatru pantheon of gods, including Tyr, Odin, Freyr, Skadi, *etc.*

· · ·

Hammerstone Kindred – This kindred group is a family-friendly group and organizes trips for members and their families to areas of interest. The members meet regularly to study and discuss Heathenry topics, including lore, mythological stories, related history, and more. The members hold numerous rituals and ceremonies to honor their gods and goddesses and share knowledge and wisdom.

Oath Keepers Kindred – This group was established by a group of high school friends in 2015 in Wisconsin, and they have small chapters all over the state.

Northern Rune Kindred – This Universalist Heathen kindred allows entry to all people regardless of caste, creed, race, gender, and any other distinction. The gods and goddesses of the Aesir and Vanir tribes are revered and worshipped. The members strive to live by the Nine Noble Virtues as they build their knowledge about Heathenism. They are based out of Herrin, Illinois.

Wyrd Ways Kindred – Based in South Jordan, Utah, this family-oriented kindred group welcomes all who seek permission to enter the fold and come with the noble intention of learning and expanding their knowledge.

Ulfr and Aesir Kindred – Based on a strict military discipline theme, this kindred believes that it is not for everyone. They practice a mixture of Asatru, combining some old ways with the new. The group is quite orthodox in its approach. Based in Missouri, this group allows entry to people of all races, creeds, genders, and communities, but you have to prove your worth over your birth.

Hrafn and Ulfr Kindred – This group has members who follow different Pagan beliefs. Some are novice Asatruars, while some others have been practicing Heathenism for many years. The members have found their way into this Heathenry kindred from Druidic paths, Witchcraft, and Native American belief systems. This kid-friendly kindred conducts blot ceremonies in open areas as often as possible. They are located in Topeka, Kansas.

Laeradr – This close-knit small community of Asatru is based out of a remote place in Norway. They are located on the island of Bjarkoy, an ancient territory of the Vikings. This island was a prominent region during the Viking Age and the Middle Ages. This kindred practices an inclusive, open-minded form of Heathenry and believes in human beings' deep connection with land spirits, gods, and ancestors.

THERE ARE many more such kindred groups, especially in North America.

Ancestors and Spirits

Since the Norse believed that those who died could continue to live and exert more power, they worshipped their dead ancestors. This tradition has been adopted and continues today, albeit with many variations depending upon the culture that holds it. But central to the belief of the Norse was the view that if the ancestors were well pleased, they would come back to protect their home and their people.

In Norse literature, we see two types of ghosts: the *haugbui* and the *draugr*. These powerful supernatural beings would guard their former possessions and haunt their community.

The haugbui was relatively harmless unless his burial mound was disturbed and deeply attached to places that were comforting to them when they were alive. Some were buried with an open grave door so that their relatives could bring food offerings, as the dead were known to always be hungry. The draugr, on the other hand, was the more malevolent ghost who haunted their family if they died in bad circumstances or were not buried properly. Some stories say they would wreak havoc in the village by killing animals and destroying property.

Gods and Goddesses Today

The Norse deities that Asatruar worship have recently become better known. Movies, comics, and TV shows have adapted various interesting gods and goddesses into mainstream pop culture. Most people are aware of the thunder god Thor, the trickster god Loki, the all-father Odin, and even the Valkyries.

Odin is the supposed leader of the Aesir gods and was also worshipped as a god of war. However, his role wasn't limited to being the god of a single aspect. Odin has been associated with various fields; he was even considered the god of poets.

The one-eyed god was also called Woden/Wotan/Wodan in various records which have been unearthed. Odin's importance can be understood by tracing the source of the word "Wednesday" as it is derived from "Woden's Day." The one-eyed Odin was considered a wise man, well-versed in magic and it is said he gained all his knowledge by hanging himself on the Yggdrasil tree for nine nights, giving up his eye in the process. Odin also married the goddess Freyja and fathered many children, including Thor.

FREYJA, also known as Friggs or Frey, is the goddess of fertility and sexuality. For this reason, she was very popular among women in ancient times. Freyja was Odin's wife, and she was the one who escorted all the fallen heroes to Valhalla along with her Valkyries. She's considered the goddess of beauty and love due to her relationship with fertility and sex. The Asatru gods are all assigned multiple roles, and they aren't limited in scope. The same can be seen in the case of Freyja, who was also worshipped as a goddess of the household because one of her roles was to protect married women.

THOR IS the single most well-known Norse god due to the various comics and movies in which he features. He's portrayed as the god of storms, which is why he was also worshipped by many in later eras when the Vikings' focus shifted to farming rather than war. Thor is depicted as an embodiment of masculine energy, and just like his mother Freyja, he is also associated with fertility. This is due to his ravenous sexual appetite and similar sexual escapades to the Greek god of thunder Zeus. Thor wields a war hammer, Mjölnir, and he was called by the other gods whenever a beast or a giant threatened the peace established by Aesir.

. . .

ANOTHER VERY POPULAR god of the Norse pantheon was Loki. Despite being an Aesir, Loki was devious and was considered a trickster god. Contrary to the popular depictions of Loki, he's not the brother of Thor or adopted son of Odin. Loki is considered to be similar to Odin in terms of stature and has also been depicted as Odin's brother in many places. He, along with the above-mentioned 3 major gods, was a major deity. It's even predicted that during Ragnarök—the Norse apocalypse, Loki would shift his allegiances and fight along-side the Jotnar to kill Odin. However, Loki wasn't an evil god by any means. He was a balancing power who questioned everything and expanded the boundaries of a society in which order was maintained by Odin and the others.

THE WAY ancient heathens viewed their deities is largely different from the ways other polytheistic religions view their gods. This holds for the modern practice of Asatru as well. In the modern world beyond this riveting ancient religion, people like to categorize things into neat boxes, and the mere attempt to mix these things is often frowned upon. It is the reason people are still fighting to keep a binary gender identi-fication or try to oppose the mixing of two races. Asatru reli-gion is not like that, and it has always been quite progressive and beyond its time. The lines in this religion continue to blur, allowing space for more ideas, better definitions, clarifi-cations, and analysis. The gods and goddesses in Asatru are rather humanistic and almost "real."

FOR EXAMPLE, Odin, who is generally known as a Norse God of War, is rarely associated with destruction or warfare in primary Asatru sources. Odin is so much more than a problematic war god that encourages bloodshed. He is associated with intelligence, wisdom, magic, poetry, and knowledge way before he is connected to war. When a modern heathen speaks of a deity, they do not assign an immortal value. They recognize that these deities have their own stories and that ancient heathens worshiped them for their unique characteristics. Being a polytheistic religion, there are so many deities that a person can connect to, depending on their personalities, desires, and characteristics. Once they spiritually connect with a heathen god or a goddess, they believe that they can communicate with them through dreams, intuitive messages, dreams, and such. Some believe that gods can directly affect the everyday happenings in their lives, and some believe that they have a broader spiritual purpose. Just like every other aspect of Asatru, it is all open to individual interpretation.

ASATRU DEITIES ARE NOT IMMORTAL, unlike many religions that worship gods. According to folklore, they perish in Ragnarok—the final destruction of the world in a conflict between deities. While some of the modern Asatru practitioners also believe in the form of Ragnarok, they consider it to be a metaphor for the many destructions in the world rather than a war of gods that would happen. According to source materials, some believe this war has already happened. They have chosen not to worship the old gods that are believed to have died during Ragnarok.

THE ALL-KNOWING and omniscient god concept also does not exist in Asatru, which is another reason it tends to attract many modern practitioners who believe in the form of deities but do not believe that they are all-powerful and all-knowing. They make mistakes just as a human would, even Odin, who is known to have the most wisdom and knowledge. He gets tricked by his wife Frigga on occasion, according to folklore. This authentic nature of portraying gods is particularly appreciated and celebrated by modern heathens, prompting even the entertainment industry to create fictional characters inspired by Norse and Asatru folklore.

Incorporating Norse Magic into Daily Life

Just as the Germanic tribes incorporated Norse magic into their daily lives, we can do the same today. To the Old Norse, magic was knowledge, as large a part of their life as possessing agrarian skills or battle skills.

NORSE MAGIC HAS ALWAYS BEEN a way to understand our place in the world and a way to create the life we want to live through our will. Magic could guide our lives and help us control it. While this is important today, it was even more important during the Iron Age and the age of the Vikings. There was always much to question. Using magic rituals to uncover your fate, make plans to change that which was ordained by the Norns was crucial. Knowing what fate had planned, you could respond in an honorable way to any challenges or even devise ways to influence or affect your life's preordained plan.

WITH THAT IN MIND, Norse magic was then and is now a way to add a layer of control and understanding to your life. The Norse people did not view their fate as something that would prevent them from exercising their free will. They believed that we could aid and construct our will to best benefit the situations ahead. There was a certain sense of freedom in not having to guess our preordained future life. Within those constraints, we could achieve great things. Magic was a way to enhance their ability to do just that.

TODAY, the use of magic easily coincides with our desire to self-actualize, to accept where we are in life, and work to make our lives better. Magic was always a way to frame and respond to challenges, which were many in the time of the Vikings. Today, we have modern medicine and healthcare and the guidance of education. Yet, the appeal and strength of magic are still very strong. Norse magic was one of the earliest recorded ways humans attempted to better control their lives and understand that the world was more than just themselves.

MAGIC HELPED the people who practiced it to protect themselves against evil, successfully handle illness, and attempt to improve relationships, both personal ones and with the land itself. With the focus on survival being both successes in battle and an agrarian life and many farmsteads and family groups isolated from one another, it was through the practice of magic, the knowledge of skilled magic practitioners, and the faith in magic's healing properties that communities could unite.

MAGIC WAS NOT ONLY the knowledge of the mystical and the natural worlds but it was also based on practical wisdom. The runic alphabet grew in use and from the desire to invoke magic. Magic led to literacy and understanding of the "other," which is located beyond the most provincial and small groups.

Fulltrúi and Ástvinr -Jotnar and Trolls and Wight

Asatru is an animistic faith. This is the belief that everything, including objects and places, possesses a certain spiritual essence. Animism believes almost everything, such as rivers, weather systems, and rocks contains a spirit or a wight. These spirits tend to be neutral towards humans; they can be pleased with offerings or angered with bad behavior.

THE WIGHTS GO by many names, such as the Huldafolk in Iceland. The Isle of Wight in England is said to have etymological connections to the Wights.

WIGHTS OR VAETTIR means land spirits, but there are also sea spirits and various other types. These different spirits of various nature-based origins symbolize the personal aspects and characteristics of nature. They represent the living, breathing attributes of nature.

SPIRITS AND WIGHTS are often used interchangeably. Historically, the wights were considered to be as important as the Gods, sometimes even more so. This was because the wights, especially the land wights, are linked to the land they inhabit. The wight's guard protects and nourishes the land and those who dwell in it, as long as they are good spirits. As humans lived on and often lived off the land by growing food, much gratitude was directed at the wights. As the wights were so closely tied to the land, it was believed that they had a much bigger say in what goes on than the Gods do. Because of their responsibility, they looked after the land the best, and gratitude was to be directed their way. This is why many revered the wights more than the Gods.

MANY WOULD PRAY to the land wights, asking for rain or healthy crops. As if those who lived on the land needed it, the wights would too. It would serve more benefit to them, so the wights would often be the first port of call to offer prayers. Many make offerings to the wights; simple offerings could include a plate of food. A few players are read over the plate and left outside. This demonstrates to the wight, goodwill, and respect. The wights are, therefore, more likely to grant requests if offered a gesture of goodwill. Honoring the wights for their everyday roles on the land keeps them in good spirits and ensures they continue protecting the land.

A LIBATION COULD ALSO BE OFFERED; this is the same as an offering but in liquid form. Once prayers are read over the liquid, it is then poured into the earth. The energy of the liquid infused with the prayers reaches the wights who live on the land. This energy infuses them with respect and honor. As a continuous offering and kind gesture, respect is shown to the land. It is recommended to avoid destroying nature or disrespecting the land. If parts of nature need to be cut down, such as a tree, for a necessary purpose. An offering should be made first, and respect is shown to all elements of nature. By disrespecting the land, the wights could be angered, and this affects their protection of the land. The wights can turn against the land and those who dwell in it as a form of punishment.

. . .

WHEN DEALING WITH WIGHTS, politeness is of the utmost importance. Dissimilar to the demons of ceremonial magic, which are dominated and can be harshly commanded, wights have free will. Wights have no reason to wish humans ill or deny help. That is unless they feel personally offended.

LAND WIGHTS ARE CONSIDERED to be the guardian spirits of the woods, streams, and forests. They tend to be friendly but prefer not to be disturbed by modern man. They are known to befriend humans and even offer help in the form of helping crows to grow and other agricultural activities. They dislike blood and violence. The Land Wights have shapeshifting abilities and can appear in various forms.

THEY ARE their strongest in the wild, as this is where they thrive due to shying away from civilized spaces. Due to their shy nature, they have easily driven away from areas which can lead to these lands failing to prosper. Land Wights usually swell in areas such as springs or rocks.

TROLLS

Some tales from Sweden describe trolls as monstrous beings with many heads who can either live in the forest and mountains or caves. The first kind of trolls that live in the mountains are known to be large, aggressive, stupid, and slow beings, always getting outwitted by the hero in the story. Those that live in caves are shy and seen as shorter than humans with stumpy arms and legs but with a fair amount of intelligence. They use the environment around them to influence their power or protect themselves and hide. These creatures emerged into mythology from the idea of the giants (jötun) in their cosmology and realms, as the word troll in Old Norse is *jätte*.

Giants

These supernatural beings of the natural world have, from the beginning of time, been the arch-rivals of the Æsir and Vanir. They often warred, fought, cheated, and married each other. The *jötun* live in the icy realm of Jötunheim, which is closely connected to Midgard by mountain ranges and dense forests, while the fire giants live in Múspellsheimr, their realm of fire. They are the catalyst of the great ending in Ragnarök, setting fire to the tree Yggdrasil and ending everything in flame.

WHAT ONE WOULD THINK of giants in physique is their immense stature, but in fact, they were no bigger than an average human and resembled the humanoid beings of other realms. They represented the original nature of chaos and destruction in comparison to the gods representing life and order.

Jotners

These are a race of giants which are separated into different categories, including frost and storm giants. It is said that Jotuns are a type of powerful creatures on the same level as Gods. Although considered giants, not all of them are big, and some are even the same size as humans. Many of the Jotuns are friendly with the Gods; however, some have friction with them. Despite this mix of friendliness and enmity, some of the Jotuns and the Gods inbreed. Uller's wife Skaoi and Freyr's wife, Gerd, are Jotuns. All of the Gods have a majority giant ancestry.

TODAY MANY VIEW the Jotuns as the biggest of the land spirits. It is now believed the Jotuns need to be helped to restore the balance instead of being battled against. Some have stuck to the traditional viewpoint that giants are inherently destructive and peace should not be made with them.

Choose the Right Path for You

Among the multiple existing Pagan religions, you can choose any path that fits your purpose. You can become a Wiccan, a Hindu, an Agnostic Pagan, or follow any other faith you like. You just have to ensure that the religion you choose is suitable for your personality and future. The point of faith is to give direction to your daily life and provide peace to your psyche.

ANSWER these questions based on the core beliefs of Paganism to figure out a direction for your belief:

Do you feel close to nature and wish to protect it?

Do you believe in the cycle of birth, death, and rebirth?

ARE you sensitive to the consequences of your actions?

. . .

Do you believe in individual moral and ethical freedom to attain peace?

Are you empathetic to the suffering of animate as well as inanimate beings?

Are you open to believing in multiple deities or one absolute God?

Have you always been fascinated by magic as a lifestyle?

Are you simply curious about the diverse faiths in existence?

Do you want to gain exposure to different cultural practices for research purposes?

If your answer to most of these questions is "yes," you agree with some fundamental beliefs of Paganism. If you are more inclined to the last two questions, you may want to become an expert or study Paganism academically. You will need to build a practical plan if you want to be a modern practitioner of Paganism.

The first step is to be specific. Avoid reading too many random sources on the internet without planning the path you want to follow. A good strategy is to research particular concepts like Wiccan rituals and Pagan traditions. Ask yourself what you are attracted to; Neo-Druidism, Shamanism, Asatru, or Green Witchcraft? Think deeply about what ideologies you have and how they match with each Pagan tradition. For example, if you care about environmental conservation and women's rights, the Neo-Wiccan or Green Witchcraft can offer you a chance to flourish. You might be an academic interested in learning about the different cultural impacts of Paganism; if that is your goal, begin streamlining your research.

A TIP for researching is to find basic facts on religion and learn about its core beliefs. This will also help you in sieving through the myths and misconceptions attached to contemporary Paganism. You must make sure your decision is based on a realistic idea of what it means to be a Wiccan or Neo-Pagan. Additionally, you must research all the Pagan beliefs, history, specific religious movements, influences, and transformations over the centuries. This will help you to make a final decision on what enamors you. You can also choose to follow multiple outlooks.

MOST PAGAN FAITHS have a process of initiation. Find out how to become a part of a coven or a community and coach yourself on specifics. You may feel uncomfortable or overwhelmed if you are unaware of the sacrifices and actions you need to take up. For instance, if you want to be a Druid, you need to go through a structured initiation process. You cannot simply initiate yourself. There are levels of achievement and criteria that must be met for your successful membership; however, you can also choose to follow an individual path and become a solitary Pagan.

. . .

IF YOU ARE STILL CONFUSED, read your sources closely. Pick up more books and do a close reading of each aspect. Ask yourself – does this make sense to you? Do you think it's ridiculous to believe in a certain aspect of the faith? Are you unclear about the topic? When you list out your fears and apprehensions, you will be able to engage in introspection better. Think about the author of the book – do you relate to them? Faith is deeply personal, and you need to make sure you relate to the community you want to join.

A GREAT TIP is to prepare a list of pros and cons. Take a piece of paper, divide it into two parts - on the left side, list pros, and use the right side to list cons. When you translate your conflicts on paper, you get a visual look into your thoughts. Having these ideas side by side will help you figure out the stakes involved in each benefit or potential harm.

YOU NEED to get a real picture of your desire to follow a certain path. You can go to the public library to read specific books. Thrift stores with second-hand books are also a good place to find specific books for study. The internet is another resource you can use to your advantage. Make sure the online resources you are referring to are legitimate and well-researched. Read book reviews and follow community threads to figure out which authors you like. Once you have built a library for yourself, you can refer to it for clarity whenever you wish. If you are still unsure about the reading list, check out study guides for beginners on sites dedicated to Paganism. It is impossible to read everything, and therefore, you should do a strategic reading. Some books might be metaphysical with tough terms and ideas. You need to spend time – develop a solid base for your intellectual concerns.

Noting down arguments that interest you – whether you agree with them or not – is a method to compile your thought process in one place.

SUCH RESEARCH WILL HELP you discover networks that will connect you to covens or groups. People who practice faith are the best resource for understanding the lifestyle of a Pagan. Finding folks with similar ideologies will help you discover a community of people and realize what you want for yourself. You can join a Meetup or go to local Spiritual stores and interact with people there. They can guide you to legitimate information. Even if you want to be a solitary practitioner, you can still approach people to brainstorm with them. Online chats and support groups can help you talk to real sorcerers and experienced magic practitioners.

HOW TO JOIN a Norse Religious Group

The Norse Faith is full of rituals and customs, which, sadly, weren't written down until long after it stopped being the predominant faith of Scandinavia and Iceland. As already mentioned, the Old Norse faith had neither a strict hierarchy nor did they rely on rigid scriptures. Today's practice is no different.

THE CURRENT PRACTICE of the Norse religion is about central ideologies such as the veneration of our ancestors and polytheism, without having strict rules on how to perform such practices. Although some congregations employ spiritual leadership, the common characteristic of the Norse faith is that it is relatively amorphous, non-authoritarian, and decentralized. However, it is not disorganized.

. . .

THE ÁSATRÚ METHOD is the best example of getting formally inducted into a Norse Adherent group (which is usually commonly referred to as a hearth or the kindred). The method of Ásatrú is as follows:

IN THE PRESENCE of a goði or gyðja and the local goðorð, the newcomer pronounces their solidarity with and devotion to the Æsir and the Vanir. Then they affirm their allegiance to the Ásatrú way of living and renounce all other religions and faiths. These affirmations are usually done on a sacred object, like an oath ring.

THE NORSE ADHERENTS are not obligated to try to convert others or to spread the religion. They openly acknowledge that the Norse faith is not suitable for everyone or universal in any way.

A GREAT WAY of getting in touch with the Asatru faith and finding your way within it is by connecting to other practitioners and heathens.

HAVING a mentor or welcoming community can help you learn more about the faith and add a certain nuance to some of the more abstract concepts and tenets of Asatru. It also gives you a sense of community and helps you transition to a heathenistic lifestyle.

. . .

SURROUNDING yourself with a supportive community also offers you companionship, which is quite important in the faith. It makes it easier to learn and grow within your faith.

COMMON PRACTICES

Are there any general practices that you could follow to start with? Of course! Numerous practices within Asatru are implemented by practitioners, although the exact methods they employ are sure to differ.

A POINT that I feel is important to make is that, as a religion, Asatru isn't much for daily practices or conversing with the gods every day. How often you practice and how you practice is completely up to you.

COMMON PRACTICES INCLUDE MAKING offerings to the gods and goddesses and perhaps prayers, but they're less common.

THAT BEING SAID, certain practices and rituals are considered quite important. In its most basic form, Asatru involves celebrating a few major festivals each year. These festivals occur on the solstices, equinoxes, and cross-quarter day, although there are a few exceptions to this rule.

Now, when you think of festivals, it would be expected to imagine these large parties that stretch throughout a town and involve the entire community. The Asatru festivals are quite different, and while they are parties, they are often more intimate affairs and are generally held among families or Asatru groups.

WITHIN ASATRU, two major types of ritual celebrations are carried out to honor the Norse pantheon. The first is called the Blot and the second is the Sumbel. Also, numerous social and cultural events may vary from practitioner to practitioner.

HERE ARE a few common ways to practice within Asatru:

THE BLOT and Sumbel

Blot is easily one of the most important practices within Asatru. Generally, when performing a Blot, a group or individual will gather in a secluded area and offer food and drink to the gods (Dees, n.d.).

THERE ARE numerous ways to perform the Blot, depending on how strictly the practitioners are focusing on the offering. Most Blot ceremonies involve a bowl of alcohol, generally mead, and this is taken as a sign that all present are partaking in the ceremony.

AFTER, it is customary to seek blessings or favors from the gods, and the rest of the mead is offered to the earth. This is the final offering.

. . .

BLOT CAN ALSO BE PERFORMED ALONE, which is great for individual practitioners. Think about a toast for a fallen soldier, pouring a drink into the fire or the ground. The same action can be performed for Blot.

SOME PRACTITIONERS MIGHT EVEN CHOOSE to perform Blot daily or at every mealtime to thank the gods for their blessing and protection.

THE SUMBEL RITUAL is very similar to Blot and involves offering food or drink. The major difference is in the intent of the ritual.

UNLIKE BLOT, Sumbel is a group ritual where the gods, heroes of old, and sometimes ancestors, are honored with offerings. It is also not so much a ritual performed for the gods, but rather it is a ritual performed in the presence of the gods.

OFTEN, a drinking horn is passed around and shared among participants so that all can drink together. According to the traditions, oaths forged during Sumbel can never be broken.

BE Active in Your Community

Now, this practice is not as 'official' as Blot or Sumbel, but the practices within Asatru rarely are. The Blot and Sumbel are key parts of practicing Asatru; they are not the only ways.

. . .

As I'VE MENTIONED, for most practitioners, Asatru is a way of life and can be practiced in various ways.

THERE IS A SAYING in Asatru that goes, 'we are our deeds.' For me, practicing Asatru forms part of every aspect of my life, and the things I do reflect my beliefs. My deeds and my beliefs cannot be separated. Nor can I separate myself, my experiences, or my perceptions from my family, my community, and my environment.

ALL OF THESE aspects make me who I am. There is a great saying that goes, 'I am because you are,' which I think perfectly encapsulates what it means to truly be part of a community. Humans, by nature, are social creatures, and the concept of community is vital to our growth and development.

IT IS in my best interest and the interest of those around me to actively participate and improve the community; however, becoming an active member of your community can be hard.

I WOULD SUGGEST you start small. Try volunteering at a local shelter or organization such as an orphanage or homeless shelter. You could also volunteer your time to help at local schools.

THE POINT IS to try to give back to the community in any way that you can. Find something that you're passionate or interested in and get involved.

. . .

Care for Nature

While not necessarily a key tenet, Asatru does focus on the importance of nature and respecting the environment. Now, as with many aspects of Asatru, this aspect is up for interpretation.

WHAT DOES RESPECTING the environment mean to you?

FOR SOME, this could mean starting a community garden or volunteering at an organization focused on conservation and nature. It could mean starting a private garden or caring for plants.

I'LL BE the first to say that I don't have a green thumb, nor am I particularly interested in plants or gardening. Therefore, when I practice, I focus on the preservation of nature. For example, cleaning up a park or beach.

CARING for nature can also be interpreted as caring for wildlife and animals. You could volunteer or work with animals.

MY POINT IS that we can honor the gods in numerous ways, and not all of them involve participating in rituals or ceremonies.

. . .

Be Careful with Your Words

Within Asatru, words hold power. They matter. The words you speak not only affect you but also the people around you. It is believed that the words you speak also affect your wyrd (your fate or destiny) as well as the wyrd of those around you.

THEREFORE, words hold immense weight and shouldn't be used carelessly.

THE IMPORTANCE of this can be seen in the weight placed on oaths and vows. To break a vow or oath is to dishonor yourself.

THEREFORE, a good way to practice Asatru is to be careful with your words. Try to be as truthful as you can, don't make promises you can't keep, and don't use your words to hurt others.

HOW YOU CHOOSE to interpret these suggestions will depend on your morals and values.

Pray

Norse Pagans don't pray conventionally, and there's no specific way to follow when it comes to praying.

· · ·

SOME PREFER to hold group gatherings and make offerings to the gods, while others prefer to do the same on their own, in private.

OTHERS PLAN and perform elaborate rituals, while some prefer just to talk.

SOME MIGHT EVEN BORROW methods and rituals from other faiths and practices.

AS THE FAITH IS DECENTRALIZED, not everyone agrees on which is the right way, but most agree that the gods are like family to them.

MOST NORSE ADHERENTS prefer not to pray with their gods in a conversational tone. This usually occurs outdoors, just like the Old Norse pagans used to. There are specific sites, like the Danish Hof Manheim, meant for rituals and ceremonies.

PERFORM *Rituals*

Many of the rituals that modern Norse pagans perform are the same as the ones Vikings and other Old Norse people performed. Some of these rituals involve:

- Honoring the gods
- Giving offerings
- Feasting together
- Raising a toast to one of the Gods
- Praying to the Gods

THE MAIN WAY of praying to the Norse gods is by focusing our thoughts on the deity we wish to invoke or by chanting prayers around a bonfire with other members of our hearth.

SACRIFICES AND OFFERINGS can be made through the blot on traditional holy days. People can also honor the Gods through their actions and words during the Sumble or a daily ritual.

IN THE OLD NORSE RELIGION, most of the festivals were inter-woven with village and farm life aspects. Survival was the ultimate goal; so, a lot of the blot or blood sacrifices were performed according to the phases of the moon to ask for a good and fruitful harvest.

THE MOST COMMON sacrifices in ancient times were animal sacrifices, but human sacrifices also occurred. The latter, though, was reserved for extreme conditions, such as war or famine. During those times, prisoners were offered to the Gods.

ARTIFACTS WERE ALSO OFTEN OFFERED, as there has been archaeological evidence in fens and bogs, such as jewelry, weapons, and tools. This method is the preferred manifesta-tion of offering in modern Norse Pagan rituals. One thing to make sure of is that none of the objects offered would harm or pollute nature.

· · ·

THE OLD NORSE used to offer mead to the Æsir. However, as mead is not very common nowadays, most modern pagans prefer to give offerings of beer or wine. Offerings aren't meant to placate the gods but to express the adherent's devotion to them.

ACCORDING TO THE LORE, Óðinn loves poetry. A good way to get Óðinn's attention is to do it in the form of a poem. All in all, the Norse's way of praying is not at all similar to what one might have in mind.

Asatru Runes and Charms as Practiced Today

Esoteric arts are a system of arts, charms, and magical culture that is connected to Asatru religion and heathenry. Many runes, incantations, charms, bands, and other magical tools are used in this particular art, and while it has faded away to some extent over the years, they are widely used even today. Runes include an advanced and magical alphabet when employed in carvings and paintings related to Asatru rituals. Divination or predicting the future is a common way modern Asatru practitioners use runes. Runic divination involves reading omens and deciphering natural signs to predict a certain good or bad outcome that may happen in the future. It also requires a lot of intuition and other magical rituals connected to the religion, such as spell work and herb magic.

RUNES AND CHARMS that come from the Asatru religion have inspired many modern spiritual practices and literature. The origin of these practices goes back centuries ago. There are stories of merchants who sailed the seas having stone tags with protective rune carvings and young lovers using runes and charms to attract their beloved. When studying folklore, the father of runes is considered to be the intelligent leader Odin, who is known for sending omens and similar signs to communicate with his followers. It is said that when Odin was learning ancient runes, the power was so great that they brought him to tears. Large volumes of ancient documents are written in runes with origins in Scandinavia, Iceland, and Germany that modern heathen continue to study and get inspiration from.

To speak of one of the most common ways runes are used in the modern era, the throwing or casting method is quite popular among the modern heathens. They keep their runes in a bag or a container. Whenever there is an issue or a situation they need a complex answer to, they focus on that issue and grab a rune from the container without looking. Then they cast or throw a handful of runes to a cloth or the altar. Then they examine the pattern in which the runes were fallen on the cloth or the stone slab and read the pattern to give themselves an idea about their situation.

Asatru is a universal and timeless religion being practiced after many centuries, relating to people authentically and spiritually. Something extremely pure and nostalgic about this ancestral religion makes it captivating to people after many years. It speaks to the purest parts of a person's heart; it is closer to nature. It allows plenty of space for analysis and interpretation, which is refreshing in a theistic religion and does not have the restrictive dogma be seen in many mainstream religions. Therefore, it is likely that people will practice Asatru many years after as a diverse, inclusive, and unrestrained religion.

THE THREE NORNIR: Urðr, Verðandi, and Skuld

A poem in the *Poetic Edda* called "Fjolsvinnsmal" refers to the Tree of Life as Mimir's Tree or Mimameid. It is also known as Lerad, a tree so huge that its twigs and leaves provide food for the goat, Heidrun, and the stag, Eikþyrnir, that live on the roof of Valhalla.

THREE ROOTS SUPPORT THE YGGDRASIL. One of these roots passes through Asgard. The second one passes through Jotunheim, and the third one goes through Helheim. The sacred Well of Wyrd where the three Norns or Nornir (the three Fates) lived was beneath Asgard's roots. Even the gods had no control over the Well of Wyrd. The Well of Mimir (or Memory), Mimisbrunnr, lay beneath the root of Jotunheim while the well Hvergelmir (or the Roaring Cauldron) lay beneath the Helheim root.

THE WORLD TREE is an essential element to the story of Ragnarok. According to prophecies in Norse mythology, only two human beings would survive the Ragnarok, namely Lif and Lifthrasir. These two people would escape from the brunt of the war by sheltering themselves in Yggdrasil's branches and consuming the dew on the World Tree leaves.

FATE AND LUCK In the ancient stories, we learn that the world and humans are fated. Some of the stories feature the *nornir*, the female spirits of fate, and while nobody knows exactly how many there are, three of them are mentioned by Snorri Sturluson and in the Eddic poem *Vǫluspá* (The *Vǫlva's* Prophecy): Urðr, Verðandi, and Skuld. The nornir live by the well called Urðarbrunnr at the foot of Yggdrasill, the tree that stands in the middle of the world and represents the cosmos. An eagle sits in its crown and a serpent lies among its roots; time flows like water through the tree, and from the crown falls the dew and rain, which flows over the world's soil and collects in the well. These three *nornir* control the fate of humans and the world. The three nornir, Urðr, Verðandi, and Skuld, represent the past, present, and future. They weave threads of fate for humans, tie them in the tree, and cut them when it is time. Skuld cuts rune-sticks for each human to set their fate and lifespan.

EVERY ÁSATRÚ GROUP and family has unique birth rituals. There is not a uniform ancient custom to refer to in modern times. However, an ancient tradition is the *nornagraut*, the *norns'* porridge. The goddesses of fate called the *nornir* are responsible for setting the fate of a human with fate-threads when they are born. This is beautifully described in the heroic Eddic poem *Helgaqviða hundingsbana in fyrri*, in stanza 3: *"Snero þær af afli ørlögþátto, þá er borgir braut í Brálundi; þær um greiddo gullin símo oc und mána sal miðian festo."*

("THEY [THE *NORNIR*] turned powerfully the strings of fate when burrows shook in Brálund [on Earth]; they tangled the golden threads and set them in the middle of the Moon's Hall [the sky].") To give the *nornir* thanks for setting a good fate for the newborn, it was an old custom (in the Faroe Islands, Denmark, and Setesdal in Norway) for the woman who had given birth to share *nornagraut* with the *nornir*. People would prepare a special porridge and the woman would share it with her married female friends, including a portion that was given to the *nornir*. The tradition also existed among the Sámi, who would prepare Sárakka-porridge for the goddess Sárakka. Both in the Sámi tradition and the Danish tradition, people would place three sticks in the porridge. In the Sámi tradition, one stick would be white, one would be black, and the third one would have three rings carved on it. The sticks would be put under the threshold of the door before nightfall, and they would tell the fortune of the mother and child based on which of the sticks had been taken during the night. There is no similar information about the Danish custom with the sticks, except that they seem to have represented the three *nornir*: Urðr, Verðandi, and Skuld.

IN THE FAROESE and Danish traditions, there is also the idea of *nornaspor*. If a child has a white spot on its nail, it is a *nornaspor* (*norn*'s mark), and it tells the fortune of the child. This has a counterpart in the Eddic poem *Sigrdrífomál*, where stanza 7 says that power-runes should be carved on the drinking horn, the back of your hand, and—to gain power-runes—you should mark your nail with *nauð*, the n-rune: n. The n-rune has been used in magic formulas since the earliest times. In an old Anglo-Saxon charm for healing, from the 11th century, it says, *"Neogone wæran Nopðæs sweoster"* ("They were nine, Nauð's sisters"). This seems to be another reference to *nornir*—here including the magical number nine, too. It is clear that the *nornir* were considered healing powers and traditionally were believed to have a hand in birth.

· · ·

THE MAIN ACTIONS TO Follow to Profess the Norse Religion

IF YOU WISH to practice Ásatrú, this is my advice to you:

- Get a good copy of the Poetic Edda and the Prose Edda.
- Get a good copy of a compilation of the Sagas of Icelanders.
- Begin experimenting with the way that you would like to connect with the gods and spirits yourself before you seek out a group. Groups can be very rewarding, but it is important to create your independent foundation for how you relate to your gods before you open up to outside influence.
- The best groups are always those based on friendship more than anything else. Real and honest friendships drive a good group of heathens much further than hierarchies and ideas of true faith.
- Always follow Óðinn's advice in the Hávamál. It will be hard to go wrong when you keep that advice in mind. They are the cumulation of hard-earned lessons through countless years, decades, and centuries.
- Always follow your heart. It is that simple.

CONCLUSION

Odin-The Father of All, Thor the Lightning God, the Great Tree Yggdrasil, the Gods' Realm Asgard, and many other myths and legends have become part of our worldwide civilization and monoculture. Such "Norse mythology" may be traced back to the ancient Nordic states of contemporary Scandinavia: Denmark, Sweden, and Norway. The most important thing to grasp about contemporary Norse mythology would be that it lacks a centralized power or "church," canonical texts, masters and hierarchies, complex theology, mandated rules or rituals, and unified standards of action and belief. Even if modern-day pagans aim to go directly to the origin more than possible — ancient Scandinavian traditions and culture — and rely on the same knowledge, it is accurate to state that each individual has their way of life, tied by similar values.

Beyond these guidelines, some people practice alone, while others do so in groups; some design their rituals, while others do not; some believe in genuine gods like Odin, while others believe that gods are parts of humanity or Jungian archetypes. Many pagans are also conscious of the impact of other revivalist religions on Norse heathenism, like Wicca or Druidry, and desire to set themselves apart from these groups.

Havamal in the "Poetic Edda" is one of the simplest short-hands for getting your mind about Norse paganism, heathenism, or whatever label you call it. Havamal is a collection of lyrical lines credited to Odin that contain guidelines on living a good, sensible life. This is significant because most pagans feel that action is more essential than faith and that what occurs after death is unimportant compared to what one does while alive.

Norse Paganism has dominated the globe recently, especially since the 1970s. Norse beliefs are known in Iceland as "satr," which loosely translates to "staying loyal to the Aesir," another of the deity families that comprise Odin, Thor, Tyr and Heimdall, according to Viking Styles. Satr is the fastest-growing state-sponsored religion in Iceland, with 3,000 adherents as of 2015. Because heathenism is not institutionalized outside of Iceland, it is difficult to gain precise figures on worldwide pagans.

In 2015, Iceland's ásatrar (followers of Satr) began construction on the Nordic country's first non-Christian church, or "hof," in hundreds of years for weddings, feasts, seasonal celebrations, coming-of-age rites, and other events. According to the Icelandic Literary Center, the Icelandic Sagas, or tales of Vikings written down in the 13th–14th centuries, have also contributed to preserving Norse paganism. If the Eddas tell stories about Norse gods, the Folk tales give us a glimpse into humans' daily lives who worship them.

Naturally, no introduction to Norse mythology would be completed without discussing runes, mystical inscriptions revealed by Odin when he sacrificed everything by hanging himself for 10 days and 9 nights on the world plant, Yggdrasil. Runes are occasionally inscribed onto objects or altars to affect a transformational result in one's life. Some pagans regard such things as facts, but others regard them as symbols, which is perfectly acceptable in heathenry.

To conclude, we can say that the book Norse Paganism for Beginners will answer every query of the interested readers. No matter what confusion you have in your mind regarding the ancient religion and its present-day application, you will get everything in the book with properly explained concepts.

Printed in the USA
CPSIA information can be obtained
at www.ICGtesting.com
CBHW071118160624
10161CB00030B/440